THE COMPLETE *Soft Coated Wheaten Terrier*

THE COMPLETE *Soft Coated Wheaten Terrier*

ROBERTA A. VESLEY

HOWELL BOOK HOUSE

New York

Maxwell Macmillan Canada
Toronto

Maxwell Macmillan International
New York   Oxford   Singapore   Sydney

Howell Book House
Macmillan Publishing Company
866 Third Avenue, New York, NY 10022

Maxwell Macmillan Canada, Inc.
1200 Eglinton Avenue East, Suite 200
Don Mills, Ontario M3C 3N1

Macmillan Publishing Company is part of the
Maxwell Communication Group of Companies.

Library of Congress Cataloging-in-Publication Data

Vesley, Roberta.
    The complete soft coated wheaten terrier / by Roberta A. Vesley.
        p.   cm.
    Includes bibliographical references.
    ISBN 0-87605-337-1
    1. Soft-coated wheaten terriers.   I. Title.
SF429.S69V47   1991
636.7'55—dc20   90-24960
                                                        CIP

Macmillan books are available at special discounts for bulk purchases for sales promotions, premiums, fund-raising, or educational use. For details, contact:

    Special Sales Director
    Macmillan Publishing Company
    866 Third Avenue
    New York, NY 10022

10 9 8 7 6 5 4

Printed in the United States of America

To my husband, Allan.
Without him this book
would not exist.

A typical display of affection by a Wheaten puppy for its young master. *A. H. Rowan*

Contents

Acknowledgments   xiii

Introduction   xv

1. What Is a Soft Coated Wheaten Terrier?   1
    The Breed Standard
    Defining the Wheaten Terrier
    The Terrier Heritage
    Is It a Watch Dog?
    The Wheaten and People
    Training and Obedience
    Health and Exercise
    Old Age
    Finding a Soft Coated Wheaten Terrier
    Wheaten Breeders
    Looking at Puppies
    What to Expect from a Breeder
    The Wheaten Coat

2. Caring for the Soft Coated Wheaten Terrier   13
    The New Puppy
    Routine Management
    Parasites
    Grooming
    The Basics

Combs and Brushes
Scissors
Other Tools
Procedure
Combing/Brushing
Bathing
Brushing
Trimming
Diet
Choosing a Food
Basic Training
Housebreaking
Jumping
Leash Pulling

3. Early History of the Breed   31
In the Beginning
The Dog in History
The Irish Connection
Terrier Origins
Early Dog Shows
The Sport of Dogs
Related Breeds
The Coat as a Distinguishing Mark
The Shipwreck Survivor
The Kerry Blue Terrier
A Different Color
A Breed Apart
Notes from The Irish Field
The 1930s
Battling Extinction
The First Club
Resisting a New Breed
The Wheaten Comes into Its Own
The Breed Is Named

4. The Soft Coated Wheaten Terrier in the United States,
   1946–1973   57
Early Imports
Early AKC Exhibition
The O'Connors
The Mallorys
The Charles Arnolds
Anne Elwell
Juanita Wurzburger

Lorraine Brownell
Dorothy Goodale
Beatrice Bossert
William F. Murray
Susan Van Allen
Constance Willis
Later Imports
The Newcomers
Interview with Maureen Holmes

5. The Soft Coated Wheaten Terrier in the United States
   Since 1974   85
   Amaden
   Andover
   Waterford
   Gleanngay
   Legenderry
   Tain
   Shandalee
   Lontree
   Brenmoor
   Wildflower
   Butterglow
   Briarlyn
   Glenworth
   Glenkerry
   Riverrun
   Crackerjack
   Clanheath
   Into the Future

6. The Soft Coated Wheaten Terrier Club of America   113
   Miscellaneous Breeds
   Getting AKC's Attention
   Forming a Club
   The Newsletter
   The Early Years
   Growth and Strife
   The First Wheaten Match Show
   Changing of the Guard
   The O'Connor Legacy
   Surviving the Challenge
   Moving Toward AKC Recognition
   The Goal is Achieved
   The First Wheaten Specialty Show

The Breeder Referral Service
Spreading the Word
Defending the Good Name
AKC Membership

7. The Wheaten in Other Countries   125
    England
      Breeders, Past and Present
      Imports from America
      The English Standard
      English Champions, 1975–1988
    Canada
      The Canadian Standard
      Canadian Champions, 1979–1989
    Wheatens on the European Continent
      Finland
      Germany
      Holland
      Sweden
      Standard of the Federation Cynologique Internationale

8. Soft Coated Wheaten Terrier Standard and Analysis   159
    General Appearance
    Size, Proportion, Substance
    Head
    Neck, Topline, Body
    Forequarters
    Hindquarters
    Coat
    Presentation
    Color
    Gait
    Temperament
    Summary

9. Breeding the Soft Coated Wheaten Terrier   179
    The Decision to Breed
    The Demand for Wheatens
    The Knowledgeable Breeder
    The Responsible Breeder
    Economics of Breeding
    Why Not to Breed—Misinformation
    Why Not to Breed—Personal Demands
    The Mechanics of Breeding
      The Brood Bitch
      Health Checks

Estrus
Shipping a Bitch
The Stud Dog
The Mating
Artificial Insemination
Is She or Isn't She?
Care of the Pregnant Bitch
Whelping
Tail Docking and Removal of Dewclaws
Weaning
Shots
Placing the Puppies
Conclusion

10. Showing Your Wheaten   195
Pleasures of Showing
How AKC Shows Work
Match Shows
Professional Handlers
Ring Presentation
Desiderata
Basic Rules
Tools
Terminology
Key Points
The Overall Outline
Complete One Side at a Time
Don't Overtrim
Legs and Feet
Grooming the Head
Coat Length

11. Wheatens in Obedience   211
How to Find an Obedience Class
AKC Obedience Titles
Tracking
Wheatens in Obedience Competition—Early Years
Obedience Wheatens Come of Age

APPENDIX 1:   Analysis of Foundation Stock Pedigrees   219
APPENDIX 2:   Local Clubs   233
APPENDIX 3:   List of Abbreviations   235
APPENDIX 4:   Wheaten Owner's Library   237

Roberta Vesley

Acknowledgments

SINCE I FIRST OWNED a Wheaten Terrier, I have met no one in dogs to whom I do not owe some debt of gratitude. They have all contributed to the knowledge and experience that culminates in the pages of this book. I cannot list all of them, but I do want to take this opportunity to acknowledge their help and to thank each and every one.

Special mention must be made of some people whose contributions became an integral part of this book. This includes everyone who provided photographs, even those whose photos could not be used because of space limitations. Sally Sotirovich provided computer printouts of the pedigrees that appear throughout the book. Her excellent database made the job a lot easier.

Marjorie Shoemaker's drawings and her discussion of ring presentation constitute an important part of the book. I thank her profusely. Thanks also to the Soft Coated Wheaten Terrier Club of America, whose publications made searching for the facts much easier. The pedigree books published under the Club's auspices can serve as a model to other clubs. I also owe a lot to Dan Kiedrowski and *Terrier Type* magazine. Dan's dedication to the Wheaten and his early interest in the breed provided a repository of historical facts that has been very useful.

The outstanding collection of material in the American Kennel

Club Library made my research much easier. The staff, especially Marie Fabrizi, constantly found items of interest and use. I gratefully acknowledge Lynn Scott for her encouragement. Under her direction, the AKC's talented art department produced the anatomical drawings and other graphic material. They deserve high praise indeed.

Thanks to my family for their helpful criticism and patience as well as their practical support in typing the manuscript. Whenever I wanted to start a new project, they gently pushed me back to the computer and "the book." Their help was invaluable.

Finally, thanks to my editor, Seymour Weiss, and the people at Howell Book House. I only regret that Ellsworth Howell did not live to see this book in print.

Introduction

IN HER BOOK *The Complete Rottweiler*, Muriel Freeman stated that she made every effort to avoid making her book a personal account. I make no such claim. The history of the Soft Coated Wheaten Terrier in America is too much a part of my own experience to separate myself from this book. The people I talk about are people I know, and many of them are my dearest friends.

My first Soft Coated Wheaten Terrier, Kelly, became a part of our family in the summer of 1969. As Lady Patricia of Windmill, she was my entrée into the world of dogs. As Kelly, she was our beloved pet, who added much to our lives while subtracting a few Barbie dolls and an occasional window screen.

Because Wheatens are so rare, the people who owned them tended to seek each other out to compare notes and share experiences. It was this coming together with other owners that started me into showing and breeding. Dog activities became a big part of my life. In 1975, I went to work for the American Kennel Club. When I became Library Director, the idea for a book about Wheatens really began.

This book is the result of serendipity at its best. It is the culmination of two decades of exciting and rewarding involvement with Wheaten Terriers. Writing it has been a labor of love. From the acquisition of a cuddly puppy twenty years ago to the more recent serious study of pedigrees and histories, it has been a gratifying experience.

Interest in Wheaten Terriers is growing steadily and I am well aware of the diversity of that interest. For the newcomer and for the prospective owner I have tried to describe the breed as accurately as possible and to be fair about both the joys and the trials of ownership. After reading the sections on care and grooming, perhaps some people will opt for another breed that makes fewer demands. Others will recognize how delightful the breed really is and will make the commitment to own, love and care for a Wheaten Terrier.

For the serious aficionado of Wheaten Terriers, here is the story of the Soft Coated Wheaten Terrier in America from its introduction to the present day. There are many breeds for which this has never been done, and for others the most recent books date from the 1920s. We are fortunate that so many of the early fanciers are still around and were willing to share their experience.

To me, the relationship of the Soft Coated Wheaten Terrier to the Kerry Blue and Irish Terriers is most important to an understanding of the history of the breed. A significant amount of attention is devoted to that history and, as with other topics in the book, information from lesser known sources has been included.

The book is a factual accounting of breed history and a guide to acquiring and caring for a Wheaten as a companion or show dog. But it is also a personal memoir. The contents of the book are based upon the facts as I found them. Some of those ''facts'' are open to question and I made every effort to balance my own personal perspective with those of others.

Extensive correspondence with fanciers throughout the world, interviews with early breeders, back issues of *Benchmarks* and *Terrier Type,* the valuable documentation in *Celebrating Ten Years of Recognition,* and the yellowed pages of old copies of *The Irish Field* have supplemented my own two decades of personal experience with Wheaten Terriers. A bibliography is provided to help the reader who wants to go further than the limited pages of this book permit.

Robert Frost's ''The Road Not Taken'' has always been one of my favorite poems. I cannot help but think how well his lines describe the evolution of this book. For me, choosing a puppy from a little-known breed twenty years ago meant following a path ''less traveled by.'' Taking that untried path has made all the difference in my life. This book is my way of sharing the story of that journey with all who have already been entranced by the Soft Coated Wheaten Terrier as well as with those whose enchantment is yet to come.

1

What Is a Soft Coated Wheaten Terrier?

WHAT IS IT that defines "character"? The word itself means "the aggregate of features and traits that form the apparent individual nature of some person or thing." Thus, we see that character involves both the physical appearance and behavior of the dog.

A breed Standard presents a "word picture" of a dog. It describes how the dog should look, how it should move and what characteristics it should not have. However, Standards do not usually cover personality to any great extent.

THE BREED STANDARD

According to the Standard for the Soft Coated Wheaten Terrier, the dog, is "a medium-sized, hardy, well-balanced sporting terrier, square in outline . . . distinguished by his soft, silky, gently waving coat of warm wheaten color . . . steady disposition . . . moderation both in structure and presentation . . . alert and happy animal, graceful, strong and well coordinated." (The Standard is discussed in depth in Chapter 8.)

This tells us what a Wheaten looks like, but beyond "alert and happy," there is little to describe the "character" of the breed.

Ch. Amaden McBuff of Sunset Hill and Amaden's Katie Love, owned by Emily Holden. *Joan Ludwig*

Wheatens make wonderful companions for children, as demonstrated here by Grants Hill Westwind and Howard and Andrew Richards. *Vic Richards*

Wheatens are not guard dogs but they are watchful of their homes and families. Ch. Crackerjacks Hallmark, ROM, owned by Sherry and Glen Yanow.

2

During the years I served as information director for the Soft Coated Wheaten Terrier Club of Metropolitan New York, the usual description of a Wheaten was "a medium-sized, blond shaggy dog that does not shed." Much of our early promotional literature used the same words. There is something about a hairy dog that appeals to people. Many Wheaten owners will openly admit that the "shaggy look" was what attracted them to the breed. The nonshedding aspect was a definite plus.

DEFINING THE WHEATEN TERRIER

But what is a Soft Coated Wheaten Terrier besides a "medium-sized, blond, shaggy dog that doesn't shed"? First of all, the Wheaten is a *dog*. This means that like any dog, it has hair, it barks at things, it jumps on people and chases cats, squirrels, balls, sticks and Frisbees.

Being a dog also means that it is a pack animal and looks to you as its leader. If you do not establish yourself as the "alpha" or head dog, you are unlikely to have a satisfactory relationship with a Wheaten. Wheatens will press to make themselves the dominant pack member but they will readily accept you as the leader if you are firm, consistent and fair.

A Wheaten is also a *terrier*. This adds another dimension to its character. Terriers do not have the best reputation among dog breeds. People think of them as noisy, aggressive and hyperactive. It takes a special type of person to own terriers. One has to accept them as they are: lively, curious and affectionate. They are strong willed and this sometimes leads people to describe them as stubborn. A quick look at their heritage helps explain this behavior.

THE TERRIER HERITAGE

The word "terrier" is from the Latin word *terra* meaning earth. These dogs were bred to go "to ground," that is, they would enter the lair of a fox, badger or rat to kill or force their prey into the open. Their lives were hard and they had to fight for whatever rewards they got.

However, terriers also lived near their masters in close quarters and thus developed their affectionate nature. Many a Wheaten owner can vouch for the fact that Wheatens go "to ground," and the holes in their backyards and gardens are ample proof. Given the opportunity, most Wheatens will catch mice and rats.

Gameness is another trait for which terriers were developed. The word means that the dog has "fighting spirit or pluck." Anyone who has stood at a show ring and watched some of the other terrier breeds has seen them "face off" and sometimes exhibit a great deal of gameness which was an essential characteristic for a dog originally intended for use on vermin.

The Wheaten is much less aggressive than other terriers. This is due to his historic use as a worker on Irish farms. Wheatens rarely start fights but will not back down when challenged. When the breed was first recognized by the American Kennel Club, a group of fanciers wanted the breed placed in the Working Group but the majority voted for inclusion in the Terrier Group, which is as it should be.

IS IT A WATCH DOG?

So here we have a medium-sized, blond, shaggy dog that doesn't shed, that goes to ground and exhibits fighting spirit and pluck. But the Wheaten is more than this. The dog is lively, affectionate, curious and alert to anything unusual. It cannot truly be called a guard dog but is definitely protective of its family and its territory. Wheatens have alerted their families to danger on more than one occasion.

When a visitor is admitted to the home, a Wheaten will accept the stranger's greeting and will most likely jump straight off the floor to offer a wet kiss. As a result, a Wheaten owner may lose some non-doggy friends. Wheatens will often circle a guest as if herding. Once a Wheaten knows you, you have a friend for life. Wheatens have long memories for friend and foe alike. While moderation is a key word in describing the Soft Coated Wheaten Terrier, the breed is far from moderate in its loyalty and affection.

THE WHEATEN AND PEOPLE

Wheatens are "people" dogs. They want to be where their family is. They do not do well in kennel situations. Wheatens are not "yappy" but will bark when there is a reason. Some tend to "talk" to their owners when they want something.

Wheatens are easy keepers. They do not require fancy furnishings. Most seek the coolness of a hard floor for sleeping. Mine constantly removed bedding from their crates, preferring to lie on the bare surface. Of course, if you encourage your dog to come up on the furniture, the animal surely will take advantage of the opportunity.

Wheatens adapt to nearly any environment. Just before I bought my first Wheaten, *New York* magazine carried an article which billed the Wheaten as "the perfect apartment dog." The size of the dog is certainly a distinct advantage for urban dwellers. The fact that the breed is not yappy is another asset to apartment living. The Wheaten's size is also advantageous for traveling.

TRAINING AND OBEDIENCE

For the most part, Wheatens are easily trained. They do well in obedience and have been successfully used as therapy dogs. With a Wheaten, as with most dogs, the important thing is to let the animal know what you want it to do. Training should be firm and consistent from the time the dog becomes part of your family.

Experts agree that behavior problems are a major reason for dogs being given up to humane societies and shelters. At present, there is a great deal of antidog feeling in this country. Every Wheaten owner must make a commitment to become a *responsible* owner. This means teaching your dog basic obedience. A well-behaved dog is a pleasure, and the time spent training is beneficial to the dog, the owner and the neighborhood.

It is vital that you establish your position as pack leader from day one. As stated above, Wheatens will jump straight up to give a greeting. This is not acceptable behavior so the puppy must be trained not to jump. Remember, that puppy will be thirty-five to forty-five pounds when grown and could injure a child or adult simply out of exuberance.

Most areas have an obedience club that offers quite inexpensive training classes. AKC can provide you with a list of clubs in your area. In lieu of or in addition to formal classes, videotapes and books are readily available. A list is included in the bibliography at the end of this book. Spend some time studying even before you get your dog. The effort you expend learning about how dogs behave before your puppy comes into your home will help make you a more confident, responsible owner.

HEALTH AND EXERCISE

The Wheaten is basically a healthy breed. Most of the breeders of the Soft Coated Wheaten Terrier Club of America (SCWTCA) are truly concerned about the breed and its future. The SCWTCA requires its member-breeders to X-ray breeding stock for evidence of hip dysplasia and to have eyes checked for progressive retinal atrophy. Cases of these conditions are uncommon, but it is only through awareness that they can be controlled.

A survey is currently underway to determine if Wheatens have significant problems with kidney disease, but at this writing the results are not available.

A moderate amount of exercise will keep your Wheaten fairly fit. However, it will absolutely thrive on regular vigorous exercise. The breed is naturally sturdy and well muscled. A Wheaten owner has to be willing to take the time and energy to provide the exercise needed to maintain good muscle tone and condition.

OLD AGE

Wheatens can be expected to live from ten to fifteen years. In old age, they may be subject to loss of sight and hearing and some arthritic problems. Cancer is not an unknown cause of death but, again, because of the small numbers of dogs involved, it is difficult to say that cancer is a major problem in the breed.

Probably the most difficult duty that comes with the territory of dog ownership is recognizing when to let go. Deciding to euthanize a beloved pet is never easy. Owners should consult their veterinarians and their own hearts as to when it should be done. There are several good books on dealing with pet loss (see Appendix 4) and reading about it is instructive and helpful.

FINDING A SOFT COATED WHEATEN TERRIER

If you have decided that you are willing to accept the responsibility of taking care of a Wheaten and all that goes with it, finding the dog of your dreams is the next logical step. The first thing to do is locate a breeder in whom you have confidence.

The American Kennel Club will supply you with the address of

Is that the mailman?   *Alan Goldie*

Wheatens get along well with other family pets.   *Charlene Adzima*

7

the parent club secretary who will, in turn, send you a list of members who are breeders. These people subscribe to the Soft Coated Wheaten Terrier Club of America's code of ethics.

You should also ask AKC for the address of a local specialty club in your area. Clubs are an excellent source of information about Wheatens. They also offer an opportunity to meet other Wheaten owners.

Be prepared to wait for the dog you want. Your breeder may not have a dog available when you are ready. Remember, you will have your dog for a long time so be patient and you will end up with the right puppy.

If you answer a newspaper advertisement, be sure to find out whether the person is a member of the national club or of a local club. Ask if he or she shows the dogs and whether they have attained any AKC titles. Involvement in a club is often a good indication that a person has more than a monetary interest in breeding dogs.

WHEATEN BREEDERS

Breeders want to find good homes for their dogs. They will ask you a lot of questions about your life-style. Some may require that if you cannot keep the dog, you return it to them. It is not unusual for a breeder to ask you to sign an agreement that covers showing, spaying-neutering, stud rights, leasing for breeding, etc. Just be sure that whatever is amenable to you and the breeder is in writing. This is for your protection as well as the breeder's.

LOOKING AT PUPPIES

When you go to see the puppies, don't be surprised to see dark brown or reddish balls of fur. The color will lighten with age. Dark shading often remains on the ears and muzzle. Some Wheatens are born very light and most breeders consider these to be "pet quality," especially if they lack pigment on the nose and foot pads.

The puppies should be lively and bright-eyed. They should be curious about you and want to be picked up. There will be some odor but you should have a general impression of cleanliness. Don't be disconcerted if the mother dog seems a bit aggressive. Her instincts tell her to protect her young. You may have to meet her in another room to get a true impression of her temperament.

8

Look for signs that the puppies are not well cared for: really long nails, unkempt coats, runny eyes and distended bellies. A responsible breeder keeps the puppies clean and well fed and sees that they have veterinary care as needed.

Do not be turned off by a breeder calling a dog a "pet." This only means that the dog is not a likely show prospect. The dog may have some missing teeth, lack pigment or have some other condition that makes it less desirable as show dog. Breeders make these decisions based on their experience with other litters. If what you want is a lovely companion, and you are comfortable with the breeder, by all means buy the puppy.

Don't be misled by what you may have heard about "pick of the litter." There is really no such thing. If the breeder plans to keep a puppy as a show prospect, you can be sure that he or she will keep the best. You will have to rely on the breeder's judgment to a great extent. He or she has lived with those puppies since they were born. Based on previous experience, he or she has a pretty good idea which one will fit best with you and your family.

WHAT TO EXPECT FROM A BREEDER

Your breeder should provide you with detailed instructions for feeding and caring for the puppy. Most breeders will give you a small supply of the food that the puppy has been eating. It is best to discuss what the puppy is eating well ahead of time so that you can have the proper food on hand.

The other things that should come with the puppy are a health record listing the shots the puppy has had, a pedigree or family tree and an application to register the dog with AKC. This blue form is what most people mean when they refer to "papers." If it is properly completed and submitted with the fee to AKC, in about three weeks you will receive a registration certificate.

Some breeders will hold the blue form for a week or ten days. This allows a period of time in which you take the dog to your vet to find out if the animal is as the breeder described. It also allows your check to clear. It is not pleasant for a breeder to deliver a dog and then have a check bounce and be left with neither dog nor money. Much of the dog game is built on faith. If you have done your homework and have good rapport with your breeder, chances are you will have a long and pleasant relationship.

Wheatens can jump straight up, and often do.   *Sue Poulin*

Two senior citizens: "Misty" (Ch. Clanheath's Misty Clover, ROM), at left, is ten and "Jody" (Ch. Andover Lucky Treasure, CD) is eleven. *Bryan McNamara*

If, by some chance, you obtain your puppy from a pet shop or an animal shelter (yes, Wheatens do turn up in pet shops and shelters) you may not get the right kind of instructions. Most dealers do not know much about the special needs of Wheaten Terriers. You should make every effort to locate other owners and breeders. AKC will refer you to the proper sources.

Some people may wish to get an older dog rather than a puppy. Breeders sometimes have mature dogs that they wish to place. If you select that option, remember the dog's basic personality is already set. You will have to do some retraining and it may take some time before close bonding takes place.

Carol Benjamin's book *Second-Hand Dog* has helpful suggestions and hints for dealing with this situation. Even if they have been abused, Wheatens respond to love and trust and can be rehabilitated.

THE WHEATEN COAT

Whether you choose a puppy or adult you should recognize that the "coat," the hallmark of the breed that first attracted you to Wheatens, is also the breed's major disadvantage. It takes regular care to keep the Wheaten coat clean, healthy and tangle-free. A matted or shaved Wheaten is not a pretty sight. The coat protects the dog from the weather and is not meant to be shaved down. Read the chapter on grooming to make sure you want to make the commitment to be owned by a Soft Coated Wheaten Terrier.

Lorry Brownell with Dungarvin of Sunset Hill and Gilchrist Gal O'Slievehoven at seven months of age.

William Gilbert

2

Caring for the
Soft Coated
Wheaten Terrier

ALL DOGS need care and training. They need to be fed, exercised and groomed. Regular veterinary visits are a must. The Wheaten is a healthy and hardy animal, and in most cases an annual visit to update vaccinations is sufficient.

The first part of this chapter is aimed at the typical one-Wheaten family. For potential owners, knowing what needs to be done to keep a Wheaten healthy and looking its best can be a factor in deciding whether they wish to make the commitment to the maintenance of a coat that requires attention on a regular basis. For most owners, the pleasure of owning a clean, well-kept Wheaten is ample reward for the effort.

THE NEW PUPPY

As soon as you know when you are bringing your puppy home, make an appointment with a veterinarian. This should be within one or two days from the time you get your dog. Ask other dog owners in the area for references. You may have to try more than one vet before you find one in whom you have confidence. You will have a very long relationship with this person, and you should be as comfortable with a veterinarian as you are with your own personal physician. It is also a good idea to find nearby emergency veterinary service. These clinics are usually open when vets are not—evenings, weekends and holidays.

Whenever you take your puppy to the vet for routine matters, leave the dog in the car until the doctor is ready to see you. Try to find someone to go with you. The waiting room may have sick animals waiting, and you don't need to expose your healthy animal to possible infection.

At your first visit, bring any records of shots that your breeder has given you. Expect the doctor to examine your puppy thoroughly. He or she should check ears, eyes, heart, lungs and abdomen. He or she may request a stool sample. If worms are present, the doctor will prescribe the appropriate medicine.

The dog will receive a program of shots over a period of months to protect it from distemper, hepatitis and leptospirosis. The doctor may also administer shots for parvo, a gastrointestinal virus. Rabies vaccine is usually given at six months of age. By the time the dog is a year old, except in case of accident or illness, your dog should only require an annual checkup for booster shots and a heartworm test.

ROUTINE MANAGEMENT

Once your puppy has been given a clean bill of health, it is up to you to keep it that way by providing an adequate diet, regular exercise, and grooming. The first thing to do is to learn what is normal for your dog. A typical Wheaten is lively and alert and has a good appetite. The eyes are clear and bright. The gums and tongue are pink and the nose is moist and cool. If these obvious signs of good health change it is time to investigate.

Observe the dog's behavior. Be aware of changes that might indicate internal parasites. If it sleeps more than usual or is lethargic, it is likely that your pet needs to see the veterinarian. Take its temperature with a rectal thermometer if you suspect a fever. The normal temperature for a dog is about 101.7 degrees. If it is 104 degrees or higher call your vet or emergency clinic. Just as a human mother almost instinctively knows when her infant is not up to par, dog owners need to accustom themselves to recognizing when their animals are not acting as they usually do.

Some things need to be checked almost daily. Pay attention to your dog's feet. Cut the hair between the pads frequently to keep the feet nice and tight and springy. Small stones and twigs can get caught in the hair and cause pain. Use blunt-nosed scissors. Accustom your puppy to having its feet handled even before much hair grows there.

Wheaten nails grow rapidly. If the dog clicks when walking on a hard floor, the nails are too long. Some dogs wear their nails down naturally. For instance, a dog that is walked on concrete or uses a cement run regularly will not need as much nail trimming as a dog that is rarely exposed to hard surfaces. If the nails get too long, the feet tend to splay or spread and the pasterns weaken.

There is a vein through the nail that is called the quick. If the nails are cut frequently and kept short, this vein recedes. The quick will bleed if it is cut. Have some kind of styptic powder on hand when doing nails. I cannot stress too strongly the importance of trimming nails weekly. (See the diagrams for instructions.)

Examine your dog's ears regularly. Remove excess hair from the ear canal. See your veterinarian if you detect an odor or if a brown waxy exudation is present. This is a sign of infection and needs professional attention before it develops into a chronic condition.

Eyes tear and matter accumulates. Regular cleaning with a moist cotton ball should prevent staining or keep it to a minimum.

PARASITES

The most common parasites that affect dogs are fleas, ticks and worms. In some parts of the country mites can also be a problem. Because it is long-haired, a Wheaten needs more careful examination to detect the presence of external parasites.

Since this book is not meant to give medical advice, dog owners have a duty to learn about potential health problems so that they can recognize them and seek proper treatment. There are numerous sources of information on the subject. A list of books can be found on page 238.

GROOMING

Routine grooming of a Wheaten Terrier is a skill that can be learned by any owner with sufficient desire and interest. The basic requirements are bathing, combing and brushing, nail cutting and trimming. Of course, trimming for the show ring is more involved and this will be discussed in a separate section.

Assuming the puppy has been obtained from a knowledgeable, reliable breeder, the animal should have had some acquaintance with the grooming table, comb, brush, scissors and nail clippers. If not, it will be up to the new owner to provide these experiences. Let us look at the "tools of the trade."

THE BASICS

The first thing to have is a grooming table. A folding one can be purchased from dog equipment suppliers or at dog shows, although it is possible to improvise. Rubber matting can be attached or placed on any solid table or surface at a height that is comfortable for you and secure for the dog. However, a grooming table is one of the best investments a Wheaten owner can make.

The table is important because the dog will associate it with grooming. Trying to groom a dog on the floor is just useless. Once a dog gets used to being on the table, it will enjoy the attention and will stand or lie down as long as is necessary. Grooming can become quite relaxing and almost therapeutic to owner and dog alike.

It helps to get the puppy used to the grooming process if you make its initial sessions short and pleasurable. While a young puppy does not have much coat, brief periods of combing and brushing help to accustom it to the sensation of being groomed. Afterward, offer a treat while the puppy is on the table. Play with the dog and praise it. Do this several times a week in the beginning.

COMBS AND BRUSHES

The Wheaten coat requires frequent combing and brushing. Steel combs with slightly rounded teeth are best. These combs are available at pet stores and dog shows.

Select a comb that feels comfortable to you. Some people like a comb with a wooden handle. I prefer a seven-inch metal comb with half of the teeth closer together than on the other half, essentially giving a medium and a fine comb in one unit. Get a good one, as combs last almost forever.

16

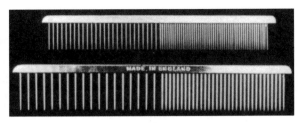

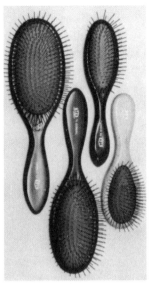

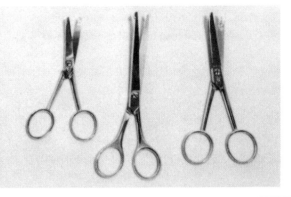

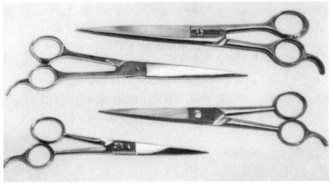

Pictured on this page are some of the grooming tools required for Soft Coated Wheaten Terriers and fully described in the text: (clockwise from top) combination combs, pin brushes, single- and double-serrated thinning shears, straight scissors and blunt-nosed shears.

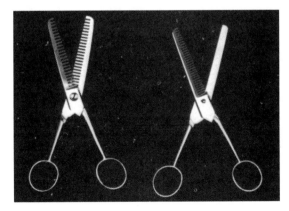

17

A pin brush with good cushioning in the base does the best job on a Wheaten coat. These brushes look like wig brushes. Most have wooden handles, but some handles are of man-made materials. The important thing is that the teeth should not be too sharp. I tried one with little protectors and found it ineffective. You may have to try several types to find the one most suitable for your dog.

A slicker brush is handy to have. It has fine wire teeth. It can be used to remove the tiny fuzz balls after you have used the regular pin brush. The slicker takes out too much coat to be used as your major brush, but it is a useful tool. The best slicker brushes have soft bristles that are gentler on the coat.

SCISSORS

You will need three different kinds of scissors: blunt-nosed, straight and thinning. Blunt or round-tipped scissors are used between the toes, on the inside of the ears and near the eyes and genitals. Although the blade points are rounded, the blades should be kept sharp.

Straight scissors are used for trimming the feet and for what I call gross trimming, that is, trimming the longest hair in order to get the beginning of the terrier outline.

Thinning shears are scissors with teeth. In some, both blades have teeth, while others have one solid blade and one with teeth. This type removes more coat at each cut. Thinning shears give a more uneven, natural look to the trimmed coat. They also thin by removing some of the hair on the spots where it grows thicker, i.e., neck, thighs, shoulders and loins. The advantage of thinning shears is that they don't leave scissor marks. Buy good quality scissors and keep them clean, dry and sharp.

OTHER TOOLS

A mat splitter is quite a useful piece of equipment. At some point, even the best-cared-for dog will develop mats. A mat splitter will break up the mat and enable you to comb it away. There are two basic types. I like the one that has about a dozen sharp blades on a handle. The blades can be replaced. This tool must be used sparingly as it does remove a lot of coat. The other kind has a curved handle and uses an injector-type razor blade. This one requires a bit more skill as it will really take out a lot of coat.

Nail clippers of some kind are an absolute must. There is a type called a guillotine and another scissors-type. An electric grinder with various attachments is also available. If you opt for automation, accustom the puppy to the noise and feel at a very early age. Some dogs just will not accept it at all. A three-sided file can be used for smoothing off the rough edges of the nail.

A Kelly forceps is not an absolute necessity but it is handy for cleaning hair out of the ears and removing ticks. It can be used to hold a cotton ball or gauze for cleaning ears or applying medication. Cotton swabs and cotton balls serve a number of purposes and should be part of your grooming kit.

PROCEDURE

Now that you have all this equipment where do you start? How do you use these unfamiliar implements? Let us begin with combing and brushing.

First check for mats. The beard, the chest, the neck, under the front legs, the elbows, the loin area and inside the thighs are the places where matting most frequently occurs.

To remove small mats, use the end of your comb in a slicing motion. When the mat is broken into ever smaller mats, you will be able to comb the hair right out from the skin or use the slicker brush. While you are working on the mat with one hand, hold the hair close to the skin with your other hand so that you are not pulling the coat and hurting the dog. Remember, grooming does not have to be a painful ordeal for you or your Wheaten.

For large mats, more drastic measures may be needed. This is where you use your mat splitters. If you use the one with the multiple blades, place it at the part of the mat nearest to the body. Slowly slice through the mat while holding the coat to minimize pulling. Make one pass at a time, then comb. As the mat is broken into smaller parts, you can revert to your metal comb and proceed as described above.

The curved mat splitter is used in a slightly different way but the result is essentially the same, i.e., making the mat successively smaller until it can be easily combed out. Hold the blade so that it enters the side of the mat and splits it in layers. Each layer can be treated separately. If your dog gets burrs or gum in its coat you may have to cut the entire mat out and possibly leave a hole in the coat. Don't be dismayed. The coat will grow back.

COMBING/BRUSHING

Now we have a mat-free animal. Begin combing the head. Comb the fall forward, being careful of the eyes. Make a part down the nose and comb the hair straight down on either side. Next, do the beard. If there is food in the hair, rub some cornstarch into it before combing.

Now proceed to the ears, neck and chest. This is where you use your brush. As you move down over the body, it may help to have the dog lie on its side. You can make yourself more comfortable if you sit on a high stool during at least part of the session. When you are doing the body, brush the coat from the skin out, working in layers. This helps remove the little fuzz balls that, untended, will eventually form mats. Be sure to always get down to the skin when you are brushing or combing.

When both sides are brushed, stand the dog and comb the coat thoroughly. While you are learning and practicing your grooming skills, you may wish to break the process into several sessions. It is important to make grooming pleasant for you and your dog. Never groom or train if you are tired and irritable. Take a break whenever you or your dog get restless.

Now that the head and body are combed and brushed, it is time for the feet and legs. These areas can be sensitive as there is not much flesh, so be as gentle as you can.

With the dog lying on its side, you can do the outsides of the legs that are on top and the insides of the legs that are underneath. Then, simply turn the dog over and repeat the procedure on the other side. You can also cut the hair between the paw pads at this point.

BATHING

Different dogs react differently to bathing. Some dogs love it, others tolerate it and still others hate every minute. My older Wheaten would get into the tub even when the bath was being run for a human. Her daughter, on the other hand, howled through the whole process and had to be held down.

Have a lot of towels and your shampoos and rinses handy. You can probably wash a young puppy in the kitchen sink or in a laundry tub. If this bothers your sensibilities, purchase some kind of tub that will hold an adult dog or use the family bathtub as most owners do. Make sure the tub has a nonslip surface. Some people even take the dog into their stall shower.

Use a shampoo meant for dogs. Many products do not irritate the eyes and can be used on both the head and body. If the dog has a flea problem, use a medicated product. (Not on the head, please.) Some good ones are available from your vet or pet supply houses.

The water should be moderately warm. You might put cotton in the dog's ears. A hand spray is a blessing for wetting the dog down and rinsing it thoroughly. After the dog is wet, work the shampoo lather through the coat completely. Pay special attention to the rear and to the feet. Don't skip the belly. Rinse thoroughly with the hand spray.

A cream rinse or detangling product can be used. Some of these must be rinsed out while others can be left in. Follow the manufacturer's directions and, if rinsing is called for, do it thoroughly.

When the bath is over, rub or blot your dog with towels until the excess water is absorbed. You can continue to use towels or put the dog on the grooming table and use a hair dryer (on low or medium setting) to hasten the process.

A Wheaten's nails are rather hard. Cutting them right after a bath is somewhat easier but the nails should be trimmed weekly. Please see the section on nails under "Routine Management" and the diagrams for instructions.

BRUSHING

As the dog dries, you can begin combing and brushing the coat. Since your dog was thoroughly combed, brushed and dematted before the bath, it should be relatively easy to do this brushing. The arrows on the diagram indicate the directions to brush. Do one side at a time with the dog lying down. Then have it stand so that you can do the back and neck. Now the dog is essentially "finished" and ready to trim. Let it rest a bit.

TRIMMING

Trimming is a skill that will improve with practice. If you are not planning to show your dog, this can be as much or as little as you care to do. However, always remember the impression your Wheaten makes on the public reflects on the breed as a whole. A shorn Wheaten is not attractive.

Even if you want to keep your dog's coat in a completely natural state, trimming must be done between the pads and around the feet, anus, genitals and ears. Too much hair on the ears prevents air circulation and can lead to infections. An overly long beard means water dripped on the floor when the dog drinks. Food can stick to the hair and cause odor. There is a certain amount of trimming that should be a part of your dog's basic hygiene. Your Wheaten deserves to be kept clean and neat.

Now you are ready to begin trimming. Stand your clean, combed-out dog on the table. Observe it from all angles and decide which areas need to be trimmed to achieve the outline you want. Placing your grooming table in front of a large mirror is most helpful for checking your progress.

Start with the head. Remove the fringe along the edges of the ears. Hold the ear so that you can feel where flesh ends and hair begins. Clean all hair from the underside of the ear using the blunt-nosed scissors. Check the ear canal for signs of infection and for excess hair in the canal itself. Gently remove the hair with your fingers or a Kelly forceps.

Cut away the hair from the area just below the ear canal to allow air circulation. Trim the outer surface of the ear with the thinning shears. Back-comb and trim with the scissors pointing up from the point of the ear. This will make it easier to blend the hair and achieve a smooth look without taking off too much coat. The ear coat should be longer at the crease than the tip so that it blends into the head coat.

In trimming the head, the idea is to achieve a rectangular look from both the top and the sides. This is done by cutting the topknot between the ears to about one and a half inches. Proceed toward the eyes, leaving the hair longer as you proceed to create the fall. The fall should not go beyond the nose. If you lift the fall and trim the area immediately over the eyes quite short, it forms a shelf which supports the longer hair and enables the dog to see better without exposing its eyes. You may also thin the hair directly over the eyes to create a veil effect.

Proceed slowly at first, taking only one or two cuts before combing the cut hair out. Never forget that the hair will grow back.

Thin the cheek area next. Cut and comb through. Do this gradually so that you do not remove too much coat. You want the cheeks to look flat, so it is necessary to thin the areas where the coat grows thick to avoid a lumpy look. Again, look at the head from all sides and trim the beard so that the look is balanced and rectangular.

The throat, neck and chest have abundant coat. These areas mat easily and are sensitive to pulling and tugging. Therefore, these sections may be thinned and tipped to a relatively short length but should never look shaved. Care should be taken to blend the coat gradually down the neck into the shoulders and topline.

Next, with the dog standing, move to the rear and determine that part of the outline. Trim the coat from the underside of the tail quite short. The front and sides of the tail should have sufficient coat to blend into the rest of the body. As a hint, from the rear, the tail should look like a little Christmas tree, with shorter branches (hair) at the top and longer ones as you proceed down the trunk (tail).

Now, trim the hair around the anus and the genitals. Continue to clear out some of the longer coat on the insides of the legs. The rear should not appear too wide. Trimming should accentuate the straightness of the legs. If too much coat is left, the dog will appear to move close in the rear.

Looking at your Wheaten from the side, begin creating a curving line with the lowest point at the elbow and the highest at the loin with a final blending into the rear leg. Comb and tip the coat. Try to make both sides match. This is where the mirror is helpful.

You can clean the hair off the center of the belly and leave the side coat to act as a curtain. This is a particularly good idea with males as it cuts down on odor from urine hitting the hair on the stomach. You can create the illusion of a dog with longer or shorter legs, depending upon how much coat you remove. Look at the dog from the top to see if there are any bulges or puffs that need additional attention and thin the coat accordingly.

The rear legs are thinned and stripped using "fluff-combing." This means using your comb to lift the coat away from the leg with a flip. You can then tip the hairs that stand outside your imaginary lines. The idea is to give a straight line from hip to ground. If you notice any bumpy areas, thin them so the line is even.

Coat tends to grow down over the rump and creates what looks like a skirt when viewed from the rear. Tip and blend carefully to achieve the desired effect. Tip and thin the hock area so that it is cylindrical from all angles. Be sure to leave enough coat on the lower leg to balance that on the front legs.

Next, we get to the front legs. The goal here is to create a column. Again, fluff-combing is the desired technique. Hair can be completely removed from the armpit area as matting occurs here. The inside of the elbow will probably need thinning. If the coat on the legs is too long its weight causes it to hang.

Finally we get to the feet. With the dog standing, use your straight scissors. Keeping them almost parallel to the table, trim the coat to create a rounded foot. Nails should not be visible protruding from under the coat. The foot should be trimmed to complete the column.

Now stand back and look at your handiwork. If it's less than perfect, don't be discouraged. It takes time to become an expert, and the coat will grow back again.

This section on grooming is designed to help the new Wheaten owner to learn the basic procedure. It is not nearly as detailed as it should be. Additional directions are in Chapter 10.

The most thorough instructions available are provided by the Soft Coated Wheaten Terrier Club of America. The official grooming chart and the *SCWTCA Owner's Manual* can be purchased from the club. (If you decide to have your local groomer do your dog, purchase a copy for him or her, too.) AKC will provide the current address of the club's secretary. Both the chart and the manual should be part of your dog library.

DIET

Dogs must eat to produce the energy needed to live. A dog's diet should contain enough fat, protein and carbohydrates to fulfill its energy needs. These needs change throughout the life of the dog. A pregnant bitch needs to be fed differently than a growing puppy or an older dog. Basically, a dog must have sufficient nourishment to make the energy it needs to maintain its 101.7-degree body temperature. Any excess energy is used for all the dog's other activities, i.e., work, play, growth etc.

Proteins, fat and carbohydrates are the main nutrients. Fat produces about twice the amount of energy as the other two. Thus, if a diet is low in fat, the other nutrients will be used to maintain basal metabolism rather than for growth, enzyme production etc. This is an inefficient way to feed.

Most breeders agree that kibble of some kind should comprise the major part of a dog's diet. Today in the United States, pet food manufacturing is a multibillion-dollar business. A dog fed on a high-quality kibble is probably better nourished than many people. These foods are generally complete diets. Much money and research goes into formulating foods that provide what a dog needs in a palatable and digestible form.

In addition to protein, fat and carbohydrates, a dog needs vitamins and minerals and water, the last being the most vital. Water helps maintain body temperature, aids in digestion, produces energy and carries the other nutrients and enzymes to the dog's cells. Without adequate water, other functions cease and the dog dies.

Protein is made up of amino acids. A dog has a minimum daily requirement (MDR) for these building blocks of life. Some are made by the dog's cells, but most come from the food the dog eats.

As stated before, fats are energy sources. They provide the means by which other nutrients enhance growth, activity, etc. Dogs store excess fat. Some excess fat is useful, but if the dog gets too much fat it will keep storing the fat and become obese. A dog only becomes too fat from consuming more calories than it uses.

Carbohydrates also furnish energy. If the dog's diet is deficient in carbohydrates, the more valuable proteins will be used to produce glucose, rather than be used for their more important work as building blocks of the cells.

Vitamins and minerals are like catalysts or triggers. They help other chemical processes to occur. Minerals are particularly important because of their effects on other nutrients.

Wheatens, contrary to some opinions, are not picky eaters. Their owners make them that way when they try to make a food more enticing by adding table scraps to it. A Wheaten, or any dog for that matter, quickly learns that if it doesn't eat every bite as soon as its plate is offered, the owner adds something to it. It is up to the owner to decide what to feed the pet. If the dog doesn't eat what is offered within ten or fifteen minutes, remove the plate and don't feed until the next mealtime. Repeat this until the dog learns that if it does not eat when you decide to feed it, it won't eat at all. No dog will starve itself.

Dogs do not need variety in their diet. They are creatures of habit and will happily and healthily exist on the same food day after day, provided it is nutritionally adequate.

CHOOSING A FOOD

When choosing a dog food, read the label. By law, ingredients must be listed in descending order according to how much of each is contained in the can or bag. Select a dry food that has at least 7 percent fat, not less than .3 percent calcium, has animal protein as one of the first four ingredients and has at least one cereal grain. Canned foods should have at least 3 percent fat, less than 78 percent water and not less than .3 percent calcium, and animal protein should be one of the first two ingredients.

While canned food is not recommended as a dog's only food, it can be added to kibble to moisten it and add that little extra taste. I prefer using boiled chopped beef or ground turkey as a flavoring.

Once or twice a week, you may add a raw egg yolk or a whole cooked egg. Eggs are a highly digestible source of protein. Liver is another excellent food that can be added to the dog's diet. Too much may cause diarrhea, so feed liver in small amounts.

When you get your puppy, your breeder will advise you about feeding. His or her advice will probably differ from other breeders and from what is suggested here. As you gain more experience, you will develop your own patterns for feeding. Be aware that you are feeding a dog, not a person, and that foods designed for dogs are best for your Wheaten and easiest for you.

BASIC TRAINING

In order to live happily with your Wheaten, you have to be willing to spend some time and effort to train your dog. The training starts when you bring your puppy home. How you treat your puppy will affect its adult behavior.

Trainers used to believe that, beyond housebreaking, a dog had to be at least six months old before it could be trained. This was probably a holdover from the days when dogs actually hunted. In recent years, much study has been done in the field of animal behavior and the current wisdom is that puppies can and should be trained to sit, stay, heel and come at an early age.

As this book is not a training manual, I will just touch on some aspects of training that the new Wheaten owner needs to know. My purpose is to outline what areas need special attention because we are dealing with Wheaten Terriers and to acquaint new owners with the responsibility that goes with dog ownership.

HOUSEBREAKING

This is the generally accepted term that means teaching your dog that inside your house is not the place for it to relieve itself. An unclean dog can become a burden to all family members and as a result may be given to a shelter or even euthanized. This aspect of your dog's training should be your top priority.

Dogs are innately clean in their habits. They do not like to eliminate close to where they eat and sleep. However, if there is a door or barrier blocking a suitable place, the dog has no choice but to use its room. Therefore, you must be there to take the dog to the place you have chosen as its toilet.

Housebreaking is easier if you establish a routine for feeding and walking. A dog needs to eliminate when it wakes and after it eats. A puppy of less than six months does not have the physical capacity to last more than a few hours without relieving itself.

A crate is an excellent aid to housebreaking and is not cruel! Dogs are den animals. They need a place of their own. A crate provides a safe haven for your puppy when you are not at home. Never use or think of a crate as punishment.

The crate needs to be large enough for an adult dog. While your Wheaten is small, you can block off part of the crate and, as the dog grows, increase the space allowed. The idea is to avoid the possibility of the dog eliminating in the crate. Do not leave a puppy under four months of age in its crate for more than an hour at a time.

Using the crate and common sense, housebreaking need not be a chore. Choose the place you want the dog to use. Even if you have a large yard, pick a small, out-of-the-way spot, take the dog there on a leash and wait until it performs. Praise it when it succeeds. If you live in an urban area, clean up after your dog. It is a simple thing to carry small plastic bags with you. Be a good neighbor.

The critical elements of housebreaking are: a crate or confined area, an established routine (don't switch on weekends just so you can sleep a little longer) and lots of praise. The effort spent in these early weeks is well worth it when the result is a clean, happy Wheaten.

JUMPING

Wheatens jump up when they greet people. Most are capable of leaping three or four feet straight off the ground to give a wet kiss. If not halted at a young age, jumping can become a serious problem and threaten the safety of people.

There are many suggested ways to stop this serious problem. One of the most sensible is given in William E. Campell's *Owner's Guide to Better Behavior in Dogs and Cats*. He tells us that dogs jump up to a person's face to smell the breath. This is generally a friendly gesture, but if your dog injures someone in its exuberance, friendliness is quite irrelevant.

Problem jumping starts when owners encourage a puppy to jump up and play. The dog cannot discriminate between acceptable and unacceptable jumping. The first step is to stop this kind of play.

Teaching your dog to sit before it gets any attention from you, including greeting, petting or feeding, is the key to solving the jumping problem. The technique can be used in other training sessions as well.

When the dog sits, praise it from a crouching position. Make the praise sufficient to reward it without overexciting it. Practice this procedure until the sit is automatic. Remember to make the dog work for whatever you give it.

LEASH PULLING

It is a pleasure to walk a dog that stays by your side on a loose lead. Wheatens are notorious leash pullers. Their necks are so strong and their heavy coats are so thick that normal leash corrections don't seem to work.

One suggested method of getting your dog to walk and heel properly is to begin the training off lead. Use a technique which is sometimes called the "jolly method."

Have the puppy off lead in a safe area. Call it to you. As it approaches, move backwards. Keep talking to it. Food treats help. Gradually get it to walk at your left side. Do this by turning away from it quickly and changing directions often until it learns to pay attention to you.

Once the puppy is working off lead, switch to doing the exercises on lead. Make leash corrections by using a quick sharp jerk and release. Perfect your skills by going to an organized obedience class. This will have the added benefit of socializing your dog.

There are other things that you have to teach your dog to make it a good canine citizen: coming when called, staying in one place and lying down. Techniques for teaching these skills can be found in many books and on videocassettes. Any basic obedience course will include these exercises. Take the time to teach your dog. You will both be better for it.

Illustration from *The Naturalist's Library,* by Lt. Col. Charles Hamilton Smith, 1854.

THE TERRIER.

Woodcut from Thomas Bewick's *A General History of Quadrupeds,* 1807.

THE TERRIER

Early woodcut of terriers hunting, from *La Venerie* by Jacques du Fouilloux.

3

Early History
of the Breed

In *The Lessons of History,* by Will and Ariel Durant, the authors state, "Most history is guessing, and the rest is prejudice." These words are particularly appropriate in a study of almost any breed of dog. Some breeds, like the Saluki and the Mastiff, have well-documented histories that date back to antiquity. When it comes to terriers in general and the Soft Coated Wheaten Terrier in particular, the matter is far from clear.

IN THE BEGINNING

There is much material in the literature of the dog about hounds and other hunting dogs and the royal lapdogs, but one must search for mention of the terriers since they did not have the status of the others. Almost every writer who addresses the history of terriers describes their origins as "being lost in the mists of time" or "obscured by myth and legend" or similar words. They are quite right.

Most authorities agree that the dog is the first animal that was domesticated by man. Archaeological evidence sets the date of the association between man and dog at least 14,000 years ago. The actual date is probably much earlier.

Many other sources put forth well-founded theories about how domestication and the process of selective breeding began. The history and origin of the dog has been studied and written about for centuries. There is a huge body of literature on the subject. In the course of searching for the roots of the Soft Coated Wheaten Terrier, we will have to examine a great deal of it.

It would be fun and romantic to imagine that dogs became domesticated the first time a Stone Age child walked into his cave with a wolf cub and said, "He followed me home. Can I keep him, mom?" That is an unlikely scenario.

When man and dog first became partners, it was as hunting companions. As other animals were domesticated for food and clothing, a man selected dogs that could help control his herds and protect them from wild predators and other tribes. The development of distinct breeds of dogs took place over thousands of years. As man progressed from being a hunter-gatherer to a food-producer to a manufacturer, he changed his dogs to suit his needs. Let us now examine the evidence.

According to Richard and Alice Fiennes in their book *The Natural History of Dogs*, "By the time written history appears, all the main groups of dogs were in existence and can be recognized from representations in stone and pottery from Egyptian, Assyrian and Greek sources." There is also strong archaeological evidence of the existence of recognizable breeds of dogs from the Mesolithic era (8000 to 2700 B.C.) in Denmark. It is pertinent to point out that the Danes were early invaders of Ireland.

THE DOG IN HISTORY

Greek writers described the different kinds of dogs with which they were familiar: Xenophon (*ca.* 434–355 B.C.) in his *Cynegetica*, Aristotle (384–322 B.C.) in *Historia Animalia* and Pliny the Elder (23–79 A.D.) in his *History of the World*. These included Beaglelike hounds for hare, dogs for hunting deer and wild boar and dogs used for war. There were no specific references to a "terrierlike" animal.

When we come to Arrian, who lived in the second century A.D., we find mention of the Celtic dogs, probably forebears of the Irish Wolfhound. Another Greek, Oppian, whose *Cynegetica* is dated about 221 A.D., gives a fascinating picture of smallish dogs used for tracking. These were bred by the "wild tribes of painted Britons" and were called "Agassaei." The dog was "round in shape, very skinny,

Reinagle engraving of terriers hunting, from *The Sportsman's Cabinet.*

Engraving showing various types of terriers, from Stonehenge's *Dogs of the British Islands.*

with shaggy hair, and a dull eye but provided on its feet with deadly claws, and it has rows of sharp, close-set teeth, which contain poison. In powers of scent the Agasseus is easily the superior of all other dogs.'' The Fienneses interpret this dog to be the ancestor of what we call terriers.

These early writers did not give us sufficiently detailed descriptions of the physical character of the dogs they wrote about for us to get a clear picture of what the dogs actually looked like. One of the first writings to give us a list of British breeds that included the terriers was *The Boke of St. Albans*, attributed to Dame Juliana Berners. It was printed in 1486 but was most likely written earlier.

In 1570 Dr. Johannes Caius published his treatise *De Cannibus Britannicus*. This work is considered to be the first book devoted to English dogs. In it, Dr. Caius gave us a classification system based on the dogs' uses and names that was accepted as a standard for over two hundred years. Abraham Fleming's 1576 English translation of this most significant work was the last English dog book published until 1800. In it, ''the Dogge called a Terrar'' is described thus: ''a sorte there is which hunteth the Foxe and the Badger or Greye onely, whom we call Terrars, because they (after the manner and custom of Ferrets in searching for Connyes) creepe into the grounde, and by that meanes make afrayde, nyppe and byte the Foxe and the Badger . . . that eyther they teare them in peeces with thayre teeth . . . or else hayle and pull them perforce out of their . . . close caves, or . . . drive them out . . .''

THE IRISH CONNECTION

Based on this evidence, we can accept the fact that a small to medium-sized keen-scented dog existed on the European continent and in the British Isles for a long time, in spite of the lack of concrete evidence. But how does this information relate to our search for the Soft Coated Wheaten Terrier?

As we have seen, the Celtic breeds were known throughout the ancient world. If we now examine a bit of known history, we can place our terriers in the proper context. Life in ancient Ireland was harsh and cruel. The island was subjected to wave after wave of invaders. Typically, these invaders settled there and became more Irish than the Irish. Their dogs most likely accompanied them and interbred with the native dogs.

The first conquerors of Ireland, in about 350 B.C., were the Gaelic Celts, a barbarian tribe from Europe. With their iron weapons, they easily overcame the primitive Bronze Age inhabitants. In 432 A.D., St. Patrick converted the Celts to Christianity. These were the years when Irish monks produced the world-famous illuminated manuscripts and books of Celtic poetry. This age of Irish glory ended with the Viking invasions in the ninth and tenth centuries. The Danes ruled until Brian Boru defeated them in 1002 to become the first and last native Christian king of Ireland.

Next came the Normans in 1170 under Henry II. Except for a few years of rule by Scotland's Robert the Bruce, Ireland was ruled by the English for the next seven centuries.

Because of this history, Ireland has been exposed to outside cultural influences. At the same time, the Irish have had an effect on their conquerors. It follows that the dogs of Ireland have been changed through various admixtures introduced by outsiders. A purist might even question whether there are really any "native Irish dogs."

One of the things that civilization by the Celts brought to Ireland was a set of laws. Unlike Greek and Roman law, which ignored them, the Brehon Tracts and the Seneachus Mor (fifth century A.D.) contained specific rules relating to dogs. These codes delineated the rights and responsibilities of dogs. They substantiate the fact that Ireland has long held its dogs in high regard. What the laws did not do was to specify breeds of dogs.

In England, King Canute (r. 1016–1035) established the first "Laws of the Forest." It is likely that the English conquerors followed these laws in Ireland as well. Under these laws, only freemen and landowners were permitted to have hunting dogs. The peasants were allowed to have small dogs that were incapable of killing large game. These dogs had to be able to fit through a ring or hoop of a specific size.

TERRIER ORIGINS

These early dogs were the ancestors of the terriers. They were small, hardy animals that kept houses and barns free of vermin for rich and poor alike and supplied the farmer's family with a steady supply of small game. These dogs were also used for menial kitchen tasks such as turning the spit. They were tough little dogs and because of their harsh life, only the strongest survived.

Illustration of an Irish Terrier, from Vero Shaw's *Illustrated Book of the Dog*. Note that the coat appears to be longer and more open than that of a modern Irish Terrier.

An early Irish Terrier, from Vero Shaw's *Illustrated Book of the Dog*.

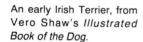

Kathleen, the first Irish Terrier shown in America in 1880 in New York. Photo from James Watson's dog book, 1905.

36

When I got my first Wheaten, the breed history claimed that the Soft Coated Wheaten Terrier had existed as a distinct breed in Ireland for at least 200 years. If we date back from the time that the Wheaten was actually recognized as a breed in 1937, we end up at 1737.

What was Ireland like in the 1700s? We know that throughout its history Ireland has been subjected to invasion—the Vikings, the Normans, the Scots, and the English. In the 1730s the English were in control and for the next hundred years their dominance continued. Irish attempts to gain independence were futile and many people were killed. The native Irish population was further reduced by the potato famine in 1845 and by mass emigration.

It is unlikely that, in that atmosphere, there was a great deal of conscientious, careful dog breeding taking place. Ireland in those days was made up of a few large cities and many hundreds of small towns and villages scattered throughout the island. Communication among villages was minimal. In such isolation, village dogs would breed together naturally and eventually would all resemble one another. Each area would have had its local dog. A dog's working ability was of great importance and its looks were secondary.

In Ireland the period after 1850 was one of relative calm. For a moment, let us return to England. This was the age of Charles Dickens. The industrial revolution was in full swing. A new class of merchants and businessmen emerged. They lived in cities, in smaller but no less grand quarters than the stately country homes of the landed gentry.

EARLY DOG SHOWS

The British are immensely fond of dogs and the nineteenth-century merchants were no different. With their newly acquired wealth, they also gained leisure time. Part of this time was devoted to gaming in the public houses. This activity often revolved around dogs. The first dog shows were held in taverns, many of which also held ratting matches. Dogs, usually terriers, were placed in a pit with rats. The best dog was the one that killed the most rats.

THE SPORT OF DOGS

When the tavern shows evolved into organized dog competitions and the Kennel Club was founded in 1873, the sport of dogs as we know it was born. The first show in 1859 was limited to Pointers and Setters, but gradually other breeds were added. When the first stud book was published by the Kennel Club in 1878, pedigrees for 4,027 dogs were included as were the results of shows and field trials dating from 1859. There were forty breeds, including fifteen different terrier breeds.

Thus was the state of the Fancy in the England of Queen Victoria. But what of Ireland? The small green island off the west coast of England is a land of legend. The Gulf Stream shields it from the frigid northern air and creates constantly changing weather. Its people are witty, charming and clannish. They are also brave and determined. These same words describe its dogs, particularly its native terriers.

In *The Dogs of Ireland*, Anna Redlich writes: "With the extinction of wolves towards the end of the century, the large hounds became scarce and smaller breeds began to take their place. The cost of living had risen and gone were the days when it was possible to feed a Wolfdog for 1½ d. per day. The netting of birds had gradually given way to the use of firearms and brought the setter to the foreground, hares were hunted instead of wolves and the smaller Greyhounds, always bred in Ireland, met the requirements of this sport. Water Spaniels now retrieved birds instead of arrows, and the kennel terrier, up to that time an anonymous vermin destroyer, attracted the interest of the sporting world."

Now, at last, here in the second half of the nineteenth century, we have our terriers *in* Ireland, at a time when dog shows are beginning and interest in controlled breeding is coming to the fore. Mendel was working on his principles of heredity in Austria. Science and technology were moving at a phenomenal rate. But where is the Soft Coated Wheaten Terrier?

RELATED BREEDS

To answer the question, we have to look at the history of the Wheaten's two cousins, the Irish Terrier and the Kerry Blue, particularly the Irish Terrier since its written history is more extensive.

There is almost no mention of the Irish Terrier in dog books before 1880. As we said previously, it was not until the early 1800s that books on dogs were common in Great Britain. H. D. Richardson did not mention the Irish Terrier in his 1857 edition of *Dogs: Their Origins and Varieties*, nor in his earlier edition of the same work in

1847, and he was an Irishman. The early dean of dog writers, J. H. Walsh, who wrote under the name "Stonehenge," did not mention the breed in his first edition (1867) of *Dogs of the British Islands*. He first discusses the breed in the third edition in 1878.

Hugh Dalziel, in his 1889 edition of *British Dogs*, states with the utmost confidence that "The breed as it now exists, has been made within the last twenty years, and that from very discordant elements." In another section he says, "to ask us to believe that the show dogs of the present day are purely descended from the Terriers of the 'Longboat' men is rather too much."

In Vero Shaw's *Illustrated Book of the Dog* (1881) the author begins the section on the Irish Terrier by commenting on the vast improvement made in the breed in the previous decade, that is, since about 1870. A well-documented dog show held in Dublin in 1876 is described by Shaw and in other major works on the dog. At this show, says Shaw, "The variety was more than charming, it was ridiculous; reports say there was no attempt at type in particular, no style; long legs, short legs, hard coats, soft coats, thick short skulls and long lean ones; all were there. 'Long, low and useful dogs' were held up for admiration. Long and useful, if you like, but never low for an Irish Terrier."

The section continues with a description of the Irish Terrier by Mr. George Krehl, vice president of the Irish Terrier Club. The first sentence of the section says, "The Irish Terrier is a true and distinct breed indigenous to Ireland, and no man can trace its origin, which is lost in antiquity. . . . Mr. Ridgeway whose name is familiar in Irish Terrier circles from having drawn up the first code of points states that they have been known in Ireland 'as long as that country has been an island,' and I ground my faith in their age and purity on the fact that there exist *old manuscripts in Irish* mentioning the existence of the breed at a very remote period." Of these manuscripts, Edward Ash in *Dogs: Their History and Development* says, "No one appears to have produced nor given the statement on which the claim of antiquity is based." Ash goes on to say, "We find that 1872, 1873 and 1874 are the years when the Irish Terrier first of all claimed attention and even then what type an Irish Terrier should be was a matter of opinion."

The last part of that sentence is quite revealing. Ash goes on to discuss an issue of the 1873 *Livestock Journal* reporting on the Dublin show that "the class for 'Irish Terriers' had no reason to be called Irish except that they had Ireland as a birth place!" In another reference to the 1876 Dublin show, he says, "Prizes had gone to long legs, short legs, hard coats, soft coats, thick short skulls, long thin skulls, and some prize winners were mongrels.''

THE COAT AS A DISTINGUISHING MARK

Of great interest to us in our search for the Soft Coated Wheaten Terrier's Irish heritage are the references to soft coats, open coats and wheaten color. About ten years later in America Charles H. Mason wrote a book called *Our Prize Dogs, Descriptions and Criticisms of the Prize Winners of 1887*. This was three years after the formation of the American Kennel Club. There are criticisms of eight Irish Terriers, four dogs and four bitches. Of Bryan Boru, a red dog, we read, ''Head coat too long; it should be short and smooth, the beard being the only hair allowable. Body-coat rather shaggy; it should be straight and close, not open.'' Of Greymount, ''Wheaten, skull rather too wide . . . neck somewhat heavy . . . coat should be straight and flat, not open nor shaggy.'' He was registered with the American Kennel Register, a registry published by *Forest and Stream*. In the bitches, two were wheaten, two red. Erin's coat was described as being ''of fair quality, but to be first class should be denser and harder.'' The others had what were considered to be proper coats.

In F. M. Jowett's *The Irish Terrier* (1933) the author notes, ''It is well-known that Irishmen, of whatever rank they may be . . . have always been noted sportsmen and there is no doubt whatever that a Sporting Terrier has been kept in Ireland for many generations, as they are referred to in old Irish manuscripts.'' (Again the unidentified Irish writings.) Jowett continues: ''They are described by an old Irish writer [anonymous?] as being the poor man's sentinel, the farmer's friend and the gentleman's favourite.'' Do these words ring a bell?

Jowett then comments on the 1874 Dublin show, noting that classes were offered for Irish Terriers over nine pounds and under nine pounds. This is an indication that size had not stabilized. Indeed, the first standard was not drawn up until 1880.

The following paragraph is most interesting and I quote it in its entirety. ''There was a large strain kept in Co. Cork, mostly Wheatens, and there was also a breed found about Ballymena and the North of Ireland which were more like the modern show Irish Terrier, being racy in type, with long punishing jaws, wheaten in color but mostly soft and open in coat.''

We find another reference to terriers with soft, open coats in the

A Scottish Terrier, from D. J. Gray's *Dogs of Scotland*.

Scottish Terrier, from *The Naturalist's Library*.

Twentieth Century Dog (1904) by Herbert Compton. He says, "Consult the various writers and compilers on the subject, and you will find the following varieties of Terriers mentioned as existing in times past, in different localities of Ireland. There was a wheaten-colored dog, high on the leg, and somewhat open in coat; there was a wheaten-colored dog, long and low on the leg, and very open in coat; there was a Terrier in County Wicklow (preserved distinct and highly prized for a century) that was long in body, short in leg and of a blue-black colour; there was a silver-haired or slaty-blue terrier in County Limerick; there was a black terrier in County Kerry; there were in different parts of the island, yellow terriers . . . red . . . black . . . black and tan . . . brindle . . . and greyish terriers . . . with smooth coats and wire coats and curley coats; there were, in short, Terrier types enough to create a collection."

The preceding excerpt is one of the earliest mentions of what was probably an ancestor of the Kerry Blue. Having brought up the subject, this is a good time to look at the breed now that we have the Irish Terrier firmly established as a distinct breed with a standard and a club formed for its protection and improvement as of 1880.

THE SHIPWRECK SURVIVOR

One of the oldest myths about the Wheaten and the Kerry is the story of the blue dog that survived a shipwreck off the coast of Ireland after the defeat of the Spanish Armada (1588). This famous traveler is purported to have swum ashore and bred with the native Wheaten Terriers to produce the Kerry. This makes for a wonderfully romantic story.

There are a number of things to ponder about this theory. First of all, would the Spanish have taken dogs with them on their journey to conquer England? They did take horses and mules to use in the hoped-for battles on land. These were dumped into the sea after the defeat by the English.

If they did have dogs with them, what kind would they have been? Some of the ships in the Armada were probably Portuguese. Is it possible that the famous blue dog was a Portuguese Water Dog? Isn't it interesting to note that, like the Wheaten and the Kerry Blue, the Porty has a single nonshedding coat that comes in a wavy variety and a curly one? Mrs. Maureen Holmes staunchly maintains that the storied blue dog was a Russian dog from a Russian ship that broke up in a storm in 1758.

I have a hard time accepting the Armada story. However, I can believe that Portuguese sailors had commerce with the Irish. Historically, the Portuguese were known for their ability as seamen. And they did take their dogs with them. They are known to have fished off the coast of Newfoundland in the sixteenth and seventeenth centuries and probably longer. They also sailed to Iceland. Ireland was a convenient place to stop for supplies and trade.

THE KERRY BLUE TERRIER

The Kerry was registered in Ireland in 1920. We have Compton's reference in 1904 to a "slaty-blue terrier in County Limerick" and a "black terrier in County Kerry." Ash mentions "a grizzle-grey-and-tan dog in the Irish Terrier classes at the Dublin show in 1876." This dog, Derby by name, had a coat that was "the texture of coconut fibre" and "an over-thick skull, and in view of the recent introduction of the Kerry Blue Terrier, this description is of some interest."

In his short section on the Kerry, Ash says, "The history of the breed is the selection from the numerous Irish Terriers to be met with there, of the best specimens, and the gradual building up of a variety by selection. Blue-coloured 'Irish terriers' were mentioned by D. J. Gray in 1887."

Ash discusses Gray's *Dogs of Scotland* at some length. In a fascinating footnote, Ash describes the cover of Part 1 of that work as having a "Scottish terrier, a dog, to modern ideas rather too long on the hind legs, and loose in coat." Ash further states that Gray "considered that the old long-legged Scottish terrier had died out, and that he had seen one of the very last, . . . that the Irish terrier was the old Scottish terrier, differing from the latter only in name"; Richardson also mentions a long-legged Scotch Terrier. Again, Ash's footnotes offer clues. The first says, "Some of these dogs were of a dark blue colour with a mixture of grey hair in the coat" and refers to the old long-legged Scotch terrier. The second one asks, "Does this explain the Kerry blue?" and refers to the statement about the Irish and the old Scottish Terriers. Things get more confused.

Ash's explanation makes a good deal of sense. There are other theories. In *Dogs: Their Origins and Varieties* (1857) H. D. Richardson wrote about a Harlequin Terrier, which later writers on the Kerry claim was an ancestor. These writers included Violet Handy and Dr. E. S. Montgomery. Dr. Montgomery also considers it a good possibility that the Kerry came from the Irish Terrier. Of the Irish he says, "they have been pure-bred in this section for nearly one hundred and fifty years. In ancient times the range of color of this breed was from dark blue to wheaten. From the latter, the Irish Terrier of the red or wheaten coat was developed; from the former came the Kerry Blue Terrier." He later states that the blue color could possibly have come from crosses with the Irish Wolfhound. He does not rule out the possibility of an admixture of Otterhound blood.

In the preface to Dr. E. S. Montgomery's *The Complete Blue Terrier* (1950) Patrick O'Neill discusses terriers he knew from his youth and states that the breed made little progress until 1925. He says the early show dogs from the years 1915 to 1925 "were, as a rule, huge, cumbersome, overlarge dogs; there were many with soft coats of poor color; light eyes were also prevalent in these years. The most successful breeders of these early dogs selected the best specimens of the Wheaten Irish Terrier for breeding; specimens of the best quality and color were bred closely and the blue variety gradually developed by selection and elimination."

A DIFFERENT COLOR

Dr. Montgomery also quotes a writer called Bennelson (1808), who describes "earth dogs" that come in all black or light gray or blue. The dogs were "strong, sturdy of body." He also described "one large terrier which was white and was strong in body and limbs . . . kept for sentiment." I have been unable to track Bennelson down and do not know whether he was Irish or English.

Dr. Montgomery relates that on a recent trip to Ireland (probably late 1940s) he talked to old men who told tales of "stone-gray terriers owned by their fathers and grandfathers." Again, we have word-of-mouth history accepted as factual. He continues by saying that the Kerry came from the Irish Terrier.

So we have now found silver-haired Irish Terriers at a Limerick show in 1887. The next reported show entry was in 1892 in Killarney for Irish Terriers (blue). The 1900 Dublin show had a Kerry shown as an Irish Terrier. In 1902, again in Killarney, a class for Blue Terriers (Working) was offered and had fourteen entries. In 1913 at Cork, classes were again offered for Irish Terriers (blue) and five were shown.

In 1916, Frank Butler, a well-known judge, described his entry of

Terri, one of the first Kerry Blue Terriers to be shown. This photo was taken at the Killarney show in 1916.

The Irish Blue Terrier as depicted in Pierce O'Connor's book *Sporting Terriers*.

twenty Blue Terriers (Working): "It certainly was a sight I had never seen before and I don't suppose I shall see the like again. The exhibits were all sized, from a small Fox Terrier to an Old English Sheepdog, and some certainly resembled the latter breed very much, most of them being blue in color. I was told that the majority of these dogs were kept for fighting purposes, so you can imagine that there was a great deal of difficulty in keeping them in anything like order, and some owners were nearly as bad as the dogs."

One of the exhibitors was a Miss Josephine Casey, who took up the breed, improved type and introduced the Kerry to England. It was registered there in 1922, largely through her efforts. There was a time lapse between the references to Kerries being shown in 1916 and 1920 when the Kerry was registered in Ireland as the Irish Blue Terrier. This was probably caused by World War I when dog activities in England and Ireland slipped to almost nothing.

The Kerry's growth in popularity in England was given a large boost when fanciers began trimming their dogs. In Ireland they are still shown untrimmed, unlike the Wheaten which is shown trimmed. Conversely, in England Wheatens are shown untrimmed.

Dr. Montgomery mentions that the breeder of the celebrated Greyhound Master McGrath (*ca.* 1866) kept the silver-gray terriers long before the Irish Terrier became popular. The dogs had curly coats. He talks of a show in Limerick in 1887 that had classes for silver-haired Irish Terriers. He then quotes Dr. Pierse, an early Kerry Blue fancier who later was responsible for the advancement of the Wheaten. "A blue terrier has existed in Ireland for centuries. . . . These terriers were of different types and had coats of varying textures, the hard or wire coat predominating, except in Kerry, where the coat was as it is today. . . . I knew Kerry Blue fanciers nearly fifty years ago, some of them being then advanced in years, and these old fanciers remembered the dog as long as fifty years before that time and in their youth knew people who had previously kept Blues for over fifty years, thus taking the records of the dog back for 150 years." At a later date, Dr. Pierse makes the same claim for the Soft Coated Wheaten Terrier.

The preceding references indicate that showing of Kerry Blue Terriers did not really take hold until the early years of the twentieth century. The Kerry was benched at a show in Cork in 1913 under the classification Irish Terriers. In 1916, in Killarney, twenty dogs were benched as "Kerry Blue Terriers." They were described as being of various sizes, some as large as Old English Sheepdogs.

The Kerry next went to England and was shown there in 1922.

English fanciers began to trim their dogs, which improved their popularity greatly and established the breed as a major contender for honors in the Terrier Group in a relatively short span.

A BREED APART

As we have looked at the histories of the Irish Terrier and the Kerry Blue, we have found mention of what must have been the progenitors of the Soft Coated Wheaten Terrier. However, it was not until the 1930s that the Wheaten attracted the interest of terrier fanciers. It is certain that wheaten-colored terriers with soft, open coats existed in Ireland in the 1800s. What is not certain is whether they existed as a separate breed or as a generic terrier as long ago as the other chroniclers of the breed aver.

The evidence clearly points to the existence in Ireland of a medium-sized light-colored terrier with a soft, open coat. During my research for this book, I relied quite heavily on the AKC library's collection of *The Irish Field,* a sporting newspaper primarily geared to horse racing. The run in the library covers the years 1931 to 1941.

NOTES FROM *THE IRISH FIELD*

Much of the information has come from a column called "Field Notes" authored by someone called "Danny Boy." He was involved in sporting terrier activities such as badger digs, ratting trials and other types of hunts. There were two organizations affiliated with the Irish Kennel Club: the Sporting Terrier Club and the Working Terrier Association. He kept tabs on, participated in and reported on their activities. He also wrote on coursing and anything else he fancied to be of interest to his readers. For example, in the January 19, 1935 issue he discusses an article on hunt terriers that appeared in the *Observer*, an English publication.

Danny quotes the *Observer*'s writer: "Many of our so-called fashionable breeds existed in their respective localities awaiting recognition. Here and there some huntsman might keep his own particular strain and breed them pure and undefiled by foreign blood. Again in some old, dark-timbered manor house, there might be a breed that had passed from squire to squire, but there were no distinct breeds with clear-cut demarcations as we of today know them."

In the same column, he includes this paragraph from the writer: "Practically unknown, except in their own country, the terrier of the olden days was of a distinct type, possessing the same attributes of sagacity, fearlessness and pluckiness which they exhibit to-day. Their breeding was kept a secret, and the old-time sportsmen were chary, indeed, of passing on their dogs to strangers. One can well understand that these old sportsmen had a cold attitude to those who would have crossed their game breed out of existence."

These two paragraphs help to explain why we find little news of the Wheaten. They also seem to support the theory that isolation kept the breed in a relatively pure state because it created a small gene pool. Local dogs bred indiscriminately and soon all resembled each other.

THE 1930s

In the search for a new "star" in the terrier world, the Wheaten was a logical candidate. Success would require defining, refining and promoting this sturdy, game and inherently beautiful animal. According to Maureen Holmes in her book *The Wheaten Years*, the rise to stardom began in 1932 when a Wheaten turned in an outstanding performance in a field trial for terriers. Several of the participants and spectators were so favorably impressed that they decided to form a club and work for recognition of the breed.

References to the Wheaten in *The Irish Field* for the years between 1931 and 1937, when the breed was recognized, are few and far between. There was no reference to the 1932 field trial mentioned above. However, it was likely that it was not an official trial because only recognized breeds could participate at Irish Kennel Club events. Since *The Irish Field* was the official voice of the Irish Kennel Club, the results of non-IKC trials would most likely not have been recorded there.

During 1932, there are almost no references to Wheatens. However, "Danny Boy" does talk about Dr. Pierse and Patrick Blake and the Blue Terriers. Trimming Kerries was debated.

In the November 5, 1932 issue, "Danny Boy" reviews a book called *Hounds and Dogs*. His comments center about the Kerry section of the book in which the author pays tribute to the value of the blood of the "Red or Wheaten" progenitors of the Kerry.

The year 1933 has many mentions of the Glen of Imaal Terrier. In the April issue, "Danny Boy" expresses fear that the Glen is nearly extinct. He asks his readers to advise him about any Imaals they may know. In the following issue, he states that people lost interest when dog fighting was outlawed as the Glen of Imal was bred primarily for fighting. An offer by a correspondent for stud service of a ''good Wheaten Glen of Imaal'' dog weighing about thirty pounds appeared in the same issue.

BATTLING EXTINCTION

In the April 15 issue, Mr. Byrne (secretary of the Working Terriers Association) also states that the Glen is nearly extinct. Two issues later, he says that he has received letters from owners of Glens and a newspaper article favoring support of the breed.

For the rest of 1933, the Glen's progress is chronicled with some regularity and the Wheaten is not mentioned. However, in the December 23 issue, ''Danny Boy'' comments on the death of a Mr. Harry Dickson. He was ''one of the truest sportsmen, sixty years in 'dogs' (of most breeds). Terriers, Greyhounds and gun dogs were his favourites—a record that might well be envied; for he was as keen a month ago as when he was a lad of sixteen. A great fancier of the Wheaten Terrier, Harry maintained that for gameness and intelligence, the dog had no equal, his own terrier, Captain, being a fine example of this contention. That dog hunted everything intelligently and, when occasion arose, as it did frequently, Captain could more than hold his own in a scrap.''

This section is interesting to us in that it is one of the first mentions of the Wheaten in a long time. Also, there is a dog called ''Captain'' that appears in old Irish Wheaten pedigrees and just dead-ends. We don't really know who that ''Captain'' was but this dog is a possibility.

Now we come to 1934. ''Danny Boy'' is writing about working terriers. Again, he mentions the Wheaten as one of the ''strong terriers'' being an expert on badgers because the dog is ''dead game.'' He also says, ''This is not the place to lament the decay of the Wheaten; some day his blood will be looked for in vain, if it be needed to ginger up the red.'' As ''Danny Boy's'' primary interest is the working terrier, he constantly derides bench show activists as being the ruin of the terrier's working ability. As the Glen of Imaal fanciers push for Irish Kennel Club recognition, ''Danny Boy'' hopes that the dog's gameness is not lost. His fear is that the ''showmen'' will tend to accentuate certain points as desirable, breeders will breed for those qualities exclusively and the dogs will move "farther away from the natural article and closer to the manufactured article." The Glen of Imaal was recognized in Ireland on May 26, 1934. The club insisted that show champions also have certificates of gameness. In November the club held its first field trials.

The next significant comments about the Wheaten are found in the July 13, 1935 issue. The first paragraph of the article says, "Some ten or twelve years ago we made an appeal in these notes for an effort to revive the Wheaten Terrier." He mentions the late Mr. Martin O'Byrne as being active in pushing for its revival.

The opening statement places Mr. O'Byrne's efforts around 1923 to 1925. Of the attempt, "Danny Boy" says, "It was apparent, even at that time, that the Wheaten had become so merged into the red Irish Terrier that there was no hope of its revival; nor could any specimens be found that would encourage the most enthusiastic."

He mentions seeing a document that referred to "The Wheaten Irish Terrier Club" and expresses interest in locating specimens. He comments that "the beautiful silky, abundant chestnut coat can be recognized by the veriest novice." He speculates that since there is a club, Wheatens must be around. But what about chestnut as a color?

The next two paragraphs are very telling: "It is close on half a century since my first association with the Wheaten Terrier and it has since been a puzzle how so admirable a dog could have been allowed to become almost extinct. If the efforts now being made are successful, the members of the club will have the good wishes and thanks of those who know what the terrier was like, and what he could do." Obviously, "Danny Boy" was not such a boy! And he places the dog as early as 1885.

THE FIRST CLUB

In her book, Maureen Holmes says that a club was formed in 1932. She lists the names of the officers. Among them were Dr. Pierse, Patrick Blake, Robert J. Bourke, John J. Clancy, Simon Doyle and Matthew Blake. In the December 7, 1935 column these same gentlemen are listed as being present at the general meeting of the Working Terrier Association of Ireland. At this meeting, the Hon. Secretary, Patrick Blake, was asked to notify the IKC that several entries had been received for the association's upcoming trial from Wheaten Terrier owners. They wanted IKC to tell them how to handle the entries. Robert J. Bourke hoped that the Working Terrier Association of Ireland would help get the breed registered.

It seems a bit odd to me that if the abovementioned gentlemen had formed a club in 1932, they did not let "Danny Boy" know about it. The Working Terrier group must surely have been a close-knit fraternity.

In any case, the entries were ruled unacceptable and the judges, Joseph Pansing and Dr. Pierse, expressed regrets. They said, "We both have known them for many years and cannot understand why such an outstanding sporting breed of terriers are not officially recognized."

In 1936, the February 2 issue discusses the effect of improved transportation. Our correspondent says, "During our peregrinations through the country we have always been on the look out for likely terriers, and, whilst we found a number of Glen of Imaal and Blue Terriers to represent the stronger breeds, we did not come across even one specimen of the old Wheaten, which, I fear, is almost quite extinct."

He goes on to say, "The craze for the Red Terrier as a bench dog may have much to do with the neglect of his forebear, the Wheaten, and there is hardly any doubt that the early characteristics of the Red as a 'fighting Irishman' were derived entirely from the Wheaten."

He also talks about Wheatens turning up in Kerry litters. He makes reference to a show where two Kerry litter brothers were exhibited. "One was whole blue and the other a pure Wheaten although shown in Blue Terrier Classes." He also speculates that both Kerries and Wheatens came from the Irish Wolfhound and "that the colour that found most favor in a given district determined the color bred for."

In the same column, "Danny Boy" notes a letter he received from a friend about the Wheaten. The friend had a Wheaten before World War I but was unable to locate one on his return.

The April 1, 1936 issue does not have a "Field Notes" column but there is a report of a meeting of the Irish Wheaten Terrier Club on April 2 in Dublin. New members were accepted. Rules and regulations were adopted along with a Standard of points for the breed. Dr. Pierse was directed to apply to IKC for recognition of the breed.

RESISTING A NEW BREED

As an example of the anti-Wheaten forces at work, the report on the General Committee's April 17 meeting is revealing. Correspondence was received by the committee from Michael Short, who objected to the name "Wheaten Terrier"; a letter of protest from the Irish Terrier Association; a letter of protest from the Glen of Imaal Terrier Club. Based on the opposition, a decision was postponed until May.

At the May meeting, a motion to accept was proposed and seconded. That motion was amended to postpone a decision for six months. A third amendment, to reject the application, was made and seconded, and rejected it was by a vote of thirteen to eight. An attempt to rescind that decision was made at the June meeting by Mr. J. D. Whittey but was unsuccessful.

The July 15, 1936 issue contained a letter from Dr. Pierse about Wheatens. He urges breeders to follow the Standard of points. He also comments that any Wheaten that looks like a modern Irish Red Terrier should be rejected. (No wonder the Irish Terrier people were so anti-Wheaten.) He also mentions that he had received numerous inquiries and that "it looks like a certainty that soon there will be a good market for Wheatens both in the USA and in Great Britain." (An article by Dr. Pierse appeared in America's *Dog World* magazine sometime in 1936. I have yet to track it down but a summary of it was in the December "Annual" issue.)

Dr. Pierse's letter brought an angry reply from R. McMullen Bolster, who claims to be "perhaps the oldest surviving member of the Irish Terrier Club." In his reply he asks the good doctor, "Incidentally, I would like to know where, in the last fifty, twenty or ten years, there has been any kennel of so-called Wheaten Terriers." He also denied prizes ever went to black and tan or gray Irish Terriers.

Dr. Pierse's reply says that he does not own Wheatens but he just does not want to see such an old Irish breed become extinct. He quotes Rowland Johns about a blue and tan grizzle Irish Terrier that won prizes. He also offers proof that gray existed in the original Irish Terrier Standard.

A report of the December 22, 1936 meeting of the Irish Wheaten Terrier Club appeared in the January 2, 1937 issue of *The Irish Field*. The club reaffirmed its commitment to seek IKC affiliation and recognition of the Wheaten.

THE WHEATEN COMES INTO ITS OWN

Thus we come to the end of the trail. The year is 1937. Wheaten interest has expanded and recognition is close. The club is well orga-

A painting of Charlie Tim.

Kingdom Leader.

nized and has the support of people highly placed in the "official" world.

Wheatens began to appear in some unofficial charity shows and in "The All Sorts of Dogs Parade." There are references to Charlie Tim, Fly Lady, Near Rover and Inchicore Boy.

In March 1937, four Wheatens took part in a badger dig. They were Short Cut, Dereen Daisy, Fenian Scout and Eagle Hill Girl.

On July 24, Dr. Pierse requested to show Charlie Tim at an IKC event but was turned down. On July 31, 1937 Charlie Tim took second place in the All Sorts of Dog Show for the "happiest looking dog." On September 4, Charlie Tim took second place in the Best Groomed Terrier class, first place as Nicest Looking Companion and fourth place in the Best in Show competition.

Finally, on September 4, 1937, the "Kennel Notes" column in *The Irish Field* announced that the Wheaten Terrier was recognized. Evidently, the meeting at which the decision was made was a long one.

THE BREED IS NAMED

The Wheaten people had already agreed to drop "Irish" from the name of the breed, but the Irish Terrier faction was not mollified. The Glen of Imaal representative was also negative and threatened to end his club's affiliation if the Wheaten was accepted. When Dr. Pierse agreed to change the breed's name to "Soft Coated Wheaten Terrier" the resolution passed by a vote of thirteen to nine.

A panel of experts was set up to pass on whether individual dogs were indeed Soft Coated Wheatens. This procedure was eliminated once a sufficient number of champions was made up. At last the Wheaten was official.

During the next ten years, ten Wheatens became champions. The breed became eligible for registration in England in 1943, even though championship status was not granted until much later. Activity in Ireland increased when Maureen Holmes became involved with Wheatens. From 1943, when she whelped her first litter, to the present, Mrs. Holmes has been a potent force in the breed.

When the breed was first accepted, it was necessary to win in field trials in order to become a champion. This requirement was eliminated by IKC in 1968.

The early history of the Wheaten Terrier is inseparable from the history of dogs in general and terriers in particular. We have followed the stories of the Irish Terrier and the Kerry Blue until we came back to the Soft Coated Wheaten Terrier. We examined facts and looked at the legends. We have brought the Wheaten to the time of its first trip across the Atlantic. While the breed is old, it is probably not as ancient as we would like to believe. A quote from Anna Redlich's *Dogs of Ireland* puts the whole thing in perspective: ''And, after all, are not the results of the evolution of a breed more important than its origin?''

Lydia Vogel with Fionn of Sonas winning the Miscellaneous class at the Westminster Kennel Club show under Louis J. Murr, February 1948.   *Evelyn Shafer*

Fionn of Sonas (right) and Joyful Jessie, the first documented Wheaten imports to the United States.   *Frederick Reuther*

4

The Soft Coated Wheaten Terrier in the United States, 1946–1973

T HE EARLIEST documented appearance of the Soft Coated Wheaten Terrier in America was in 1946. Prior to that date, there is almost no mention of the breed in this country. We have noted the description in the *American Book of the Dog* (1889) of the wheaten-colored Irish Terriers with soft, open coats. A "yellow north of Ireland Terrier" was shown at Westminster in October 1878, a show which is not recorded with AKC. These dogs could have been Wheatens but we cannot be sure.

EARLY IMPORTS

What we can be sure about are the imports of 1946. They arrived by boat on November 23 and were consigned to Miss Lydia Vogel of West Springfield, Massachusetts.

The dogs were Fionn of Sonas (Cheerful Charlie ex Wheaten Lady) and Joyful Jessie (Dawson Lad ex Auchinleck). The next recorded imports were received by Mr. and Mrs. J. T. O'Brien of Washington, D.C., Holmenocks Hallinan (Holmenocks Highlander ex Ir. Ch. Handsome Hallmark of Holmenocks) and Holmenocks Hydova (Holmenocks Kismi Hardy ex Ir. Ch. Handsome Hallmark of Holmenocks).

In her book *The Wheaten Years*, Maureen Holmes mentions two other dogs that were sent to the United States. Holmenocks Kismi Hardy (Glenguard Mournside Firecrest ex Elegant Eileen of Holmenocks) and Anner Rose (Silver Whiskers ex Anner Bell) went to Indiana. Unlike Fionn of Sonas and Joyful Jessie, they were never registered with the Soft Coated Wheaten Terrier Club of America.

The next exported dogs that she tells us about are Gads Hill, born in April 1956 (Ir. Ch. Melauburn ex Ir. Ch. Holmenocks Herald), and a bitch, Holmenocks Hallmark, whelped in May 1956 (Ir. Ch. Melauburn ex Holmenocks Hilite). They were consigned to Mrs. Ann Hagan Howland but eventually became the property of the Charles Arnolds of Connecticut.

Their call names were Liam and Maud. Liam sired the famous 1962 Fourth of July litter out of Holmenocks Gramachree (Ir. Ch. Holmenocks Hartigan ex Griselda), who was owned by the O'Connor family. This family's interest in the breed is discussed later in this chapter. Earlier this pair produced a litter while the Howlands lived on Block Island. Those puppies were never registered and were given to friends. The Arnolds got one.

EARLY AKC EXHIBITION

Miss Vogel began to show her dogs at AKC shows in the Miscellaneous class and approached the American Kennel Club to request recognition. According to correspondence in AKC's files, she was advised that it would take more than two Wheatens to achieve acceptance. Somewhat discouraged, Miss Vogel continued to show and breed but placed the majority of her puppies as pets.

The records for most of the dogs she bred have been lost. There were seventeen dogs involved. Berlyd Belle of Dublin, whelped in August 1947, and two of her offspring, Bo Peep of Berlyd Acres and Daisey of Berlyd Acres, whelped in 1951, were registered retroactively in the SCWTCA Stud Book.

Lydia Vogel showed Fionn and Jessie in the Miscellaneous class at Westminster in 1947. This was the first time Wheatens were exhibited in the United States as far as is known for sure.

First known litter of Wheatens to be whelped in the United States, in August 1947.

Frederick Reuther

Rev. Tom O'Connor with one of the Gramachree dogs. *Finn's Studio*

THE O'CONNORS

About ten years later, Margaret O'Connor of Brooklyn, NY, came across a picture of a Soft Coated Wheaten Terrier in a paperback book *The New Book of Dogs* (Maco Magazine Corporation, 1954). Information in Margaret's files identifies the dog as Fionn of Sonas, Lydia Vogel's dog.

She contacted the publishers and located Lydia, who had no puppies but who put her in touch with other owners. Ultimately, through Mr. O'Brien of Washington, D.C., she was able to contact Maureen Holmes in Ireland. As a result the O'Connors welcomed Holmenocks Gramachree (Ir. Ch. Holmenocks Hartigan ex Griselda) into their lives on July 30, 1957. She was immediately dubbed "Irish" by Margaret's father.

In 1961, with some trepidation, Margaret showed Irish at the Staten Island Kennel Club show. This was the first time a Wheaten had been shown in over ten years. The experience was so satisfying and the interest she experienced so great that she decided to try locating other Wheaten owners.

At first only the Charles Arnolds were interested in the project of working toward AKC recognition, but Margaret could be persuasive and her enthusiasm for the breed was contagious. A dozen or so owners were finally located. On March 17, 1962, a small group met at Ida Mallory's home in Brooklyn and started the Soft Coated Wheaten Terrier Club of America.

The objective was to protect and preserve the Soft Coated Wheaten Terrier in the United States. Margaret worked in public relations and used her skills in promoting the Wheaten. She started a club newsletter which she sent to twelve subscribers. The second issue in August 1962 went to fifty people. (See Chapter 5 for details of the club's history.)

Margaret cajoled Dan Kiedrowski, publisher of a fairly new monthly magazine known as *Terrier Type*, into accepting a breed column on Wheatens. She rarely missed a month from September 1963 until her untimely death in May 1968. Her mother, Mrs. A. Cecelia O'Connor, continued writing the column through 1971. The O'Connor family's unfailing devotion to the breed was communicated through these columns.

In 1965 Margaret authored *How to Raise and Train a Soft Coated Wheaten Terrier* (TFH Publications). Now out of print, it was the only source for breed history until Maureen Holmes wrote *The Wheaten*

The July 4, 1962, litter whelped by the O'Connors.   *Courtesy Rev. Tom O'Connor*

A historic trio, these Wheatens are (from left) Holmenocks Gramachree, CD, Gramachree's Minute Man, CDX, and Gramachree's Little Firecracker, CD.

Evelyn Shafer

Years in 1977. *How to Raise and Train a Soft Coated Wheaten Terrier* is now considered a collector's item.

In addition to writing about Wheatens, Margaret with her sister, Eileen Jackson, and their brother, Tom, a Jesuit priest, showed in the Miscellaneous classes and Obedience. In her *Terrier Type* columns and in *Benchmarks*, the official publication of the SCWTCA, Margaret urged Wheaten owners to get their dogs before the public by showing in breed and/or Obedience. Eileen joined Charlie Arnold with Maud and Liam and showed Irish at the last Westminster show that offered Miscellaneous classes in 1963. Margaret also managed to get newspaper coverage and television appearances for her dogs.

The O'Connors became active exhibitors in Obedience. Eileen showed "Rory," Gramachree's Minute Man (Gads Hill ex Holmenocks Gramachree, CD), to his CD title on December 20, 1964 at the Bronx County Kennel Club with a score of 192. Rory was the first Wheaten to gain an AKC Obedience title. He finished his CDX title in 1966. Fr. Tom O'Connor eventually became an AKC Obedience judge and was instrumental in promoting the idea of allowing handicapped exhibitors to participate in Obedience Trials.

Holmenocks Gramachree completed her CD at the Bronx County Kennel Club in October 1965 at the age of eight and a half years. She became the first Wheaten bitch to earn a CD title. According to Fr. Tom and Margaret, Irish seemed to learn from watching the other dogs practicing. It took only five sessions at the Suffolk Obedience Training Club, and she earned her first leg at the Ox Ridge Kennel Club show in Darien, Connecticut.

Her daughter, Gramachree's Little Firecracker (sired by Gads Hill) finished her CD at Queensboro in 1966. Cracker was the fourth Wheaten to get a CD title. Faraderry Fairy (Garfield Highball ex Holmenocks Halcyon) was the third Wheaten to gain a CD title.

After Margaret's death, her family continued the work she started. They followed her record-keeping system and kept showing dogs but primarily in Obedience. They imported dogs for others. A litter out of Faraderry Fairy and Minute Man was whelped soon after Margaret died. This was the last litter to carry the Gramachree name. The dogs the O'Connors bred and imported formed the American foundation of the Soft Coated Wheaten Terrier.

One of the most important actions taken by the O'Connors and the newly formed club was the establishment in 1965 of the Soft Coated Wheaten Terrier Club of America Stud Book. The records were retroactive to the first dogs imported by the O'Connors and eventually

Irish Ch. Melauburn.

Charlie Tim
Cheerful Charlie
Lambay Heroine
Mourneside McCoul
Silver Leader
Silver Wheat
Wheatielocks
Holmenocks Handley
Warspite
Blonde Bomber of Holmenocks
Tipp Sally (Tipperary Sally)
Holmenocks Hazel
Glenguard Mournside Firecrest
Holmenocks Halo
Glenguard Erris Lady
Melauburn
Silken Paddy
Glenflesk Captain
Ashen Blonde
Glenguard Mournside Firecrest
Cheerful Charlie
Cheerie Be
Golden Gleam
Holmenocks Hunch
Charlie Tim
Cheerful Charlie
Lambay Heroine
Handsome Hallmark of Holmenocks
Silver Leader
Silver Wheat
Wheatielocks

included records on Fionn of Sonas and Joyful Jessie. There were over 1,100 dogs listed when the Stud Book was finally submitted to AKC in late 1972.

There is no doubt that the O'Connors did their part in working toward recognition. Fr. Tom and his mother were active in the breed until after its recognition by AKC. Rev. O'Connor judges regularly at AKC Obedience Trials and was a member of the Obedience Advisory Committee.

THE MALLORYS

Ida Mallory lived near the O'Connors and they became friends. Ida had always been involved in dogs, usually working for humane societies. At this writing, she lives in Maine and manages a local animal shelter. Ida helped teach Margaret about breeding and whelping puppies. She also helped with club work and correspondence.

Her husband, Louis, taught at Brooklyn College and when he retired in 1964, they moved to Maine where she continued her work with animals. In those years in Brooklyn, the Mallorys were known for using hand-finished dog crates as end tables.

The Mallorys' kennel name was Grant's Hill. Their foundation bitch was Gramachree's Independence (Gads Hill ex Holmenocks Gramachree). They were the first to exhibit Wheatens at the Vacationland show in Maine. They also promoted the breed on television and to other dog clubs.

The Mallorys did not breed extensively but they managed to place dogs in states where the breed was not already found. The Mallorys helped to achieve wider geographic distribution of Wheatens, an AKC requirement for acceptance. Grant's Hill Wheatens were sold to people in Ohio, Colorado, Pennsylvania, Washington and California.

In addition to Independence, the Mallorys imported a bitch in whelp, Holmenocks Hailsworth (Holmenocks Hackney ex Holmenocks Henrietta). From the resulting litter sired by Holmenocks Halyard (Melauburn ex Holmenocks Hilite) the Mallorys kept two puppies, Grants Hill Downeaster, a dog, and Grants Hill Westwind, a bitch. Downeaster was bred back to his dam and produced a bitch, Grants Hill Ocean Melody, who was sent to Dorothy Goodale in Colorado. She was one of the foundation bitches for Mrs. Goodale's Berdot Kennels.

A 1965 litter out of Holmenocks Halyard and Holmenocks Hailsworth, bred by Ida
Mallory. *Vic Richards*

Ida and Louis Mallory with
Gramachree's Indepen-
dence.
Vic Richards

THE CHARLES ARNOLDS

As noted, Gads Hill and Holmenocks Hallmark were sent to America to Ann and William Howland. The Arnolds met Maud and Liam in 1957 at the Howlands' home on Block Island. They produced a litter that year which was never registered. The Arnolds got a bitch that they called Shamrock I. When the Howlands divorced, Ann asked the Arnolds to take Liam and Maud, which they happily did.

In 1962, the Arnolds received a call from Margaret O'Connor, seeking a stud dog for Irish. Maggie and Ida Mallory drove to Cobalt, Connecticut, to meet Liam. He was, to quote Charlie, "irrepressible" and at the time absolutely ungroomed. In spite of appearances and Charlie's description of Liam's lack of experience, the two ladies from Brooklyn decided he would do.

Later that year, on St. Patrick's Day, the Arnolds with their dogs were in New York to see their daughter march with her class in the parade. They made a side trip to Brooklyn to visit the Mallorys and the O'Connors. It was during this meeting that the SCWTCA was founded.

In May, Irish was bred to Liam. The aforementioned Fourth of July litter was the result of that mating.

In November of the same year, the Arnolds had their first litter out of Liam and Maud. The breeding was accomplished with the aid of a veterinarian. It produced Katie O'Cobalt who produced Gallagher of Sunset Hill. Gallagher went to Constance Willis (Hopping Brook). In 1968, Katie was sold to Susan Van Allen (Brenock Wheatens).

After her success at Staten Island, Margaret pestered Charlie and Eileen until they agreed to try showing. Liam's coat had been completely cut down when he was bred to Maud and it was just beginning to grow back. Nevertheless, he was entered at the Westbury show. He went into the ring truly looking like a blond Kerry and won. He continued to win in other shows. He was six years old at the time.

The Arnolds changed their kennel from Cobalt to Sunset Hill when they moved to a new home. The name became well-known in the breed and they bred and showed extensively. Dogs of their breeding became foundation stock for Andover Wheatens (Jackie Gottlieb and her daughter, Cindy Vogels) and the Slievehoven line (Anne Elwell) among others.

The Arnolds imported an English dog, Binheath Perro Benito (Kelly of Binheath ex Kilndown Macushla), who was widely used at stud. One of his daughters, Thistledown of the Egerluk (ex Pride of

A group of Wheaten puppies. Note the variation in coat density and texture.

Two puppies from the 1957 litter bred on Block Island by Ann Hagan Howland. The litter was not registered. The Arnolds' Shamrock I is in the foreground. Hero is in the background. Gads Hill was the sire, Holmenocks Hallmark the dam.

Marrethays bred by the William Murrays) produced foundation stock for Waterford (Dan and Marjorie Shoemaker) and Lontree (Joy Laylon). Both owned Cloverlane bitches out of Thistledown.

Another daughter, Muffin's Miss Muffet, was sold to Barbara Luks. She in turn produced Ch. Lady Colleen of Forest Glen when bred to Ch. Stephen Dedalus of Andover, CD, ROM. In 1975, Colleen was bred to Ch. Mellickway Crackerjack, ROM, and produced Ch. Crackerjacks Hallmark, ROM.

One of Perro's sons, Brenock's Kelly's Lucky Charm, was also a popular stud. His offspring influenced the following lines: Shandalee (Sue and Harvey Goldberg) through Hogan of Hopping Brook, Erinmore (Jack and Marcia Cohan) through Slievehoven's Country Squire, Glenkerry (Mary Pickford) through Slievehoven Western Traveler, Elfinstone (Linda Wolters) also through Squire, Glenworth (Karen Worth) through Harrigan of Hopping Brook, Gilchrist (Lorry Brownell) through Gilchrist Gal O'Slievehoven and Amaden (Emily Holden and Carol Carlson) via Jenny Love of Addison Mews.

Another Perro son, Shamrock O'Perro O'Brandy Keg, sired the first litter bred by Nina Cassel out of her foundation bitch, Legenderry's Dervorgael. He also sired Donegal's Master Kerry out of Cloondora of the Egerluk who was owned by Frank Maselli (Templemore).

In 1963, the Arnolds imported two Irish-bred dogs from Mrs. George Bourke. These littermates figure predominantly in many of the early American pedigrees. Cobalt Bourtor Ballynilty and Cobalt Bourcro Ballybay were out of Holmenocks Grand Coup ex Croom Crespina. Another bitch out of the same litter, Croombour Crackerjill, was sent to Jean Free. She was the dam of Ch. Innisfree's Annie Sullivan, ROM, the breed's first Best in Show winner.

The Arnolds were extremely important in the development of the Wheaten in America. Charlie was active in the SCWTCA from its beginnings through the years leading to recognition. The Arnolds showed regularly and bred dogs that influenced many of today's prominent lines. Although they no longer show or breed, at this writing they still have one old Wheaten bitch to whom they are extremely devoted.

ANNE ELWELL

Anne Elwell once owned a shaggy blond dog which had come from an animal shelter. Somebody told her it looked like a Wheaten Terrier. When the dog died, Anne decided to try finding a Wheaten

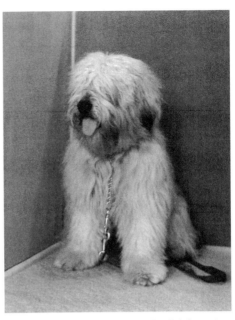

Cobalt Bourtor Ballynilty in 1964 on Block Island. He was imported from England by the Arnolds.

Binheath Perro Benito, the English import.

Head study of Gads Hill by Carolyn Hales.

purebred. The Arnolds had an ad for puppies in *The New York Times*. She called and ended up with Callahan of Sunset Hill (Cobalt Bourcro Ballybay ex Holmenocks Hallmark) in 1965.

She purchased Toby Mug of Sunset Hill (Gallagher of Sunset Hill ex Cobalt Bourtor Ballynilty) in 1968. She also owned Sliebhoben Lady Anne Gregory (Towhead Charlie of the Egerluk ex Holmenocks Hildegarde) and Brydie of Balitara (Benker Belton ex Gramachree's Eivlin Aruin).

Toby Mug was bred to Brenock's Kelly's Lucky Charm in 1969 and produced Gilchrist Gal O'Slievehoven, who joined Gilchrists Galley Gal (Towhead Charlie of the Egerluk ex Kerry) at the home of Richard and Lorry Brownell. They became the foundation of the Gilchrist Wheatens.

Slievehoven's Country Squire was produced from a repeat of the same breeding in 1971. He was owned by Jack and Marcia Cohan and was important to the Erinmore line.

Anne Elwell's influence on the progress of the Wheaten was not only based on her breeding. She introduced a number of future important breeders to Wheatens. Among these were Lorry Brownell, Carol Carlson, Emily Holden, Marjorie Shoemaker and Gay Sherman.

Anne Elwell also showed extensively. In her travels, she met Horace "Jud" Perry, a noted Kerry Blue breeder/handler. He had little respect or affection for Wheatens or their owners. However, Anne was able to win him over. Jud shared his knowledge of structure and movement with her. He agreed to take Toby Mug to the International Kennel Club show in Chicago provided he could "trim her up a bit." Reluctantly, Anne agreed. However, Jud took her two weeks early to get her used to him.

The dog had already been entered at another show and when Toby Mug turned up trimmed, "all hell broke loose" among the Wheaten people. Some exhibitors advised the judge that trimming was not permitted under the Standard and that a protest would be made if the bitch was placed.

How much this affected the judge's decision is not certain but Toby did not place. However, she did take first place in a large class in Chicago. Thus began the trimming wars.

JUANITA WURZBURGER

Juanita Wurzburger's first Wheaten was Marretthay's Irish Colleen (Ir. Ch. Holmenocks Hamish ex Golden Moss), imported from

Charles Arnold, showing Ch. Sunset Hills Padraig O'Cara at the Manhattan Savings Bank Dog Show in 1976. Note the trimming.

Toby Mug of Sunset Hill won the Miscellaneous class in 1970 at Chicago International under Hollis Wilson. She was handled by Judd Perry. Note the extreme trimming.　　　　　*William Gilbert*

Anne Elwell showing Brenock's Kelly's Lucky Charm in 1970.　　　*Evelyn Shafer*

71

County Cork in 1965. Bred to Gramachree's Minute Man, she produced Leprecaun's Top Shoemaker. Owned by Peter and Judy Siegel, he won Best in Match at the first Soft Coated Wheaten Terrier match ever held.

Juanita also imported Holmenock's Hispaniola (Holmenocks Hackney ex Holmenocks Henrietta). Known as "Rooney," she was also bred to Gramachree's Minute Man, CDX, and produced Leprecaun's Jackeen Arrah (John) and Leprecaun's Mistress Maggie. "John" was the sire of Ch. Stephen Dedalus of Andover ("Sweeney"), one of the breed's most important sires. More than 1,500 of the dogs that eventually became AKC champions in the early years after recognition trace back to Leprecaun foundations through Sweeney.

Leprecaun's Mistress Maggie's November 1968 record litter of twelve puppies, sired by Tanjybairn (Cobalt Bourco Ballybay ex Cornbin Tanjareen), provided Ruth Stein (Raclee) with her foundation bitch, Leprecaun's Golden Heather. Raclee's best known offspring is Ch. Raclee Express West O'Andover, CD, ROM.

Leprecaun's Golden Elf and Leprecaun's Lovely Colleen were produced by a Hispaniola–Jackeen Arrah breeding. Colleen was the dam of the author's foundation bitch, Lady Patricia of Windmill who produced Ch. Mellickway Crackerjack, ROM (by Ch. Stephen Dedalus of Andover, CD). Elf was used by Audrey Weintraub on Tammara of Balitara to produce Legenderry's Ainlee, CD, ROM, a top producing bitch.

Juanita Wurzburger's contribution in the early years is unquestioned. Not only did she breed a number of important dogs, but she also taught others about breeding. She encouraged people who got dogs from her or through her referrals to show and to breed.

Juanita served as secretary for the parent club for many years. She wrote occasional columns about Wheatens in *Dog World* magazine. Those who knew her remember her with great fondness even though they did not always agree with her.

LORRAINE BROWNELL

The Brownells were almost the only early Wheaten owners who knew anything about dogs or showing. They raised German Shepherd Dogs and owned a boarding and training kennel. Lorry just wanted a small dog that she could show on her own. The Shepherds were too much for her to handle. She located a woman who had some Wheaten puppies, and she and a casual friend each bought one.

Marretthay's Irish Colleen, owned by Juanita Wurzburger.

Lady Patricia of Windmill, owned by the author. Her best-known offspring was Ch. Mellick Way Crackerjack, ROM.

The dogs had been kept in a rather dark, gloomy cellar. No matter what Lorry did, she was never able to train the puppy. To this day, she thinks the dogs had some sort of psychological problem caused by lack of socialization. She called her "my yo-yo dog." She eventually placed the dog on a farm. Several years later, she met a woman with a male who acted in the same way. It turned out to be a litter brother to the yo-yo.

Lorry continued her search for a good Wheaten, but some breeders refused to sell to her because she ran a kennel. All this changed after she met Anne Elwell at a dog show. She credits Anne with providing her with over twenty years of pleasure and happiness with Wheatens. Through Anne, she got Gilchrists Galley Gal and Gilchrist Gal O'Slievehoven.

Lorry Brownell's Gilchrist name appears in the pedigrees of some important dogs. Her foundation bitch, Gilchrist Gal O'Slievehoven was whelped in November 1969. Bred to Dungarvin of Sunset Hill, Galley produced Ch. Gilchrist's Dena of Waterford, one of the first bitches owned by Marjorie Shoemaker.

A repeat breeding produced Ch. Gilchrist's Echo O'Braemara, CD, owned by Marcia Moore of Cheyenne, Wyoming. Lorry also owned Dungarvin of Sunset Hill (Gallagher of Sunset Hill ex Cobalt Bourtor Ballynilty) and Amaden's Bendacht, out of Dungarvin and Jenny Love of Addison Mews (Brenock's Kelly's Lucky Charm ex Roscommon's Uncommon of Sunset Hill).

DOROTHY GOODALE

Dorothy Goodale bred many Wheatens during the time she was involved in the breed. She bought dogs from a number of different lines. Her Berdot line was based on a relatively small number of dogs.

In males she owned Gramachree's Deoch an Dorais (Gramachree's Minute Man, CDX, ex Faraderry Fairy, CDX), Bennekerry Beechnut (Holmenocks Hancock ex Hurley's Lass), who she sent to Emily Holden in 1972, and Katie's Doctor Dhu Little (Gramachree's Roderick Dhu ex Sunset Hills Kilkenny Kate).

Her foundation bitches were Blarney Blondie, an Irish import by Holmenocks Hancock out of Honeycub Golden Dawn, and Grants Hill Ocean Melody (Grants Hill Downeaster ex Holmenocks Hailsworth).

Mrs. Goodale's very tight linebreeding produced Berdot's Brigette (Katie's Doctor Dhu Little ex Berdot's Peg O' Our Hearts)

Marretthays Marshallat, originally owned by Mrs. Mary Jane Robey, was later sold to Bea Bossert.

The House of Patria

Ch. Stephen Dedalus of Andover, CD, ROM. "Sweeney" was the most influential early sire. He appears in nearly every Wheaten pedigree.

Andover Antic of Sunset Hill, CD, owned by Cynthia Vogels, is best known as the dam of Ch. Stephen Dedalus of Andover, CD.

who was the dam of Ch. Abby's Postage Dhu O'Waterford, ROM. Her littermates, Berdot's Toby Lad and Berdot's Sabrina Fair (Katie's Doctor Dhu Little ex Amy's Wearin' the Green), were sold to Donna Henseler who based her Riverrun Kennel on them. Linda Shroer of Pioneer Wheatens also began with Berdot stock.

BEATRICE BOSSERT

Bea Bossert lived in Wisconsin and purchased two Wheatens from the O'Connors, Gramachree's Cruiskeen Lawn (Bourcro Bantry Bay ex Gramachree's Little Firecracker) and Gramachree's Magread A Chara (Gramachree's Minute Man, CDX, ex Faraderry Fairy, CDX). She also imported Holmenocks Hallahuna (Holmenocks Grand Coup ex Holmenocks Hailsworth) and became the second owner of Marrett-hay's Marshallat (Holmenocks Hamish ex Golden Moss). Mrs. Bossert bred a few litters and was instrumental in promoting the Wheaten in the Midwest during the 1960s.

WILLIAM F. MURRAY

Bill Murray imported Pride of Marretthays (Holmenocks Hamish ex Golden Moss). He bred her to Cobalt Bourcro Ballybay in 1965 and she produced Little Mermaid of the Egerluk who went to Sue Van Allen. Pride was also bred to Binheath Perro Benito and produced Thistledown of the Egerluk, Marilyn Carens's foundation bitch. Marilyn Carens bred the Cloverlane bitches that became foundation stock for the Waterford and Lontree lines. Bill bred a few more litters but they did not lead to any major lines.

SUSAN VAN ALLEN

Susan Van Allen started her breeding with Little Mermaid of the Egerluk. Mermaid was bred to Binheath Perro Benito three times. Sue bought him from the Arnolds in 1968. One of the males from the first litter, Shamrock O'Perro of Brandy Keg, was sold to Tina Tryon.

He was used by Nina Cassel in her first breeding of Legenderry's

Dervorgael. That breeding resulted in two champions, Ch. Tain's Brigadier Gerard, owned by Virginia Potter (Chermar), and Ch. Tain's Sir Nigel Loring, who belonged to Jerry Stifelman and Ian McDermott (Jason Wheatens).

Sue kept a bitch, Brenock's My True Kerry Love, from the same litter. Kerry was bred back to her sire and produced Sweet Molly Malone, who was the dam of Ch. Duffy Muldoon. Duffy was owned by Alice Papaliolios (Butterglow).

Sue showed her dogs and continued breeding into 1976. She was active in the Central New York Kennel Club and served as the club's secretary for a number of years.

CONSTANCE WILLIS

Constance Willis was Charlie Arnold's sister-in-law. In 1968, Mocara of Sunset Hill was transferred to her. When she first started breeding she kept the Sunset Hill name, but later she used Hopping Brook as a kennel name. She also owned Gallagher of Sunset Hill (Cobalt Bourcro Ballybay ex Katie O' Cobalt) who, when bred to Mocara, produced O'Callahan of Sunset Hill, the sire of Ch. Innisfree's Annie Sullivan, ROM.

Although Mrs. Willis did not breed many litters, some of the dogs that trace back to her breeding have had an important effect on the breed. Harrigan of Hopping Brook (Brenock's Kelly's Lucky Charm ex Mocara of Sunset Hill) bred to Cissy Caffrey of Andover resulted in Ch. Glenworth's Country Squire, ROM. Hogan of Hopping Brook also added greatly to Sue Goldberg's Shandalee lines.

LATER IMPORTS

As so many dogs were being bred here by the late 1960s, imports were few. A significant one, from England, was Binheath Cushlamacree (Binheath Winston of Finchwood ex Kilndown Macushla). Bred to Grants Hill Yankee Trader, she produced Lady Gregory of Longridge, who was the foundation bitch of Alice Papaliolios's Butterglow Kennel. Lady Gregory produced Ch. Butterglow's Dream Weaver, ROM, the first bitch to win a SCWTCA National Specialty in 1976.

Bryan and Mary Lynne Reynolds imported Ch. Holmenocks Halpha, who added greatly to the Ballynacally breeding program by producing Ch. Ballynacallys Brydie Tyrrell, ROM. The Reynolds were concerned that the Wheaten was losing its Irish character and imported Halpha to reinforce the traits in the Ballynacally line.

In 1965, Nancy Selz imported Holmenocks Histora, a littermate to Juanita Wurzburger's Hispaniola. She bought Gramachree's Dermod O'Derry (Gramachree's Minute Man, CDX, ex Faraderry Fairy, CDX) from the O'Connors. He was born in March 1966. She bred a number of litters under the kennel name Sonsai.

THE NEWCOMERS

As the number of Wheatens increased, new people came into the breed. They began to show in Breed and Obedience throughout the country. Margaret O'Connor, and later her mother, reported the show wins in *Terrier Type* and *Benchmarks*.

The newcomers commenced breeding activity and the Wheaten grew in numbers. In her June 1966 column, Margaret reported that over 115 Wheatens were registered with the Soft Coated Wheaten Terrier Club of America. In 1968, a year after Maggie's death, nearly 250 Wheatens were listed, with dogs reported in twenty states.

The year 1968 was a high point in the struggle for AKC recognition. This was the year Jackie Gottlieb began showing Andover Antic of Sunset Hill (Cobalt Bourcro Ballybay ex Katie O'Cobalt). It was not Maggie's show record that started the final and successful push toward recognition but rather the interest, enthusiasm and organizational skills of Jacqueline Gottlieb that galvanized the scattered fanciers into a unified group with one goal in mind. Jackie knew how to get people to participate.

More and more people were getting involved. From New Jersey, Anne Elwell was showing Toby Mug of Sunset Hill (Gallagher of Sunset Hill ex Cobalt Bourtor Ballynilty) and Callahan of Sunset Hill (Cobalt Bourcro Ballybay ex Holmenocks Hallmark). Carol Carlson showed Roscommon's Uncommon of Sunset Hill (Gallagher of Sunset Hill ex Mocara of Sunset Hill).

Long Island was a major center of Wheaten activity. Judy Siegel showed Leprecaun's Top Shoemaker (Gramachree's Minute Man, CDX, ex Marretthay's Irish Colleen). Audrey Weintraub brought out Tammara of Balitara, CD (Benker Belton ex Gramachrees Eivlin Aruin).

Mary Pickford with Slievehoven Western Traveler and Betsy Finley with Ch. Sweeney of Sunset Hill, the first Soft Coated Wheaten Terrier to win a Terrier Group. *Lloyd Olson*

Some of the entries in the Open bitch class at the October 1973 Mongomery County Kennel Club show. They are (from left) Jerome Podell with Ch. Kate Dedalus of Forest Glen, Linda Wolter with Ch. Glenkerry the Phantom, CD, Emily Holden with Ch. Jenny Love of Addison Mews, Aileen Schafer with Ch. Slievehoven's Irish Mist, CD. *Evelyn Shafer*

Suzanne Bobley worked in Obedience and conformation with Gramachree's Roderick Dhu, CD (Gramachree's Minute Man, CDX ex Faraderry Fairy, CDX). He was known as Max and gave his name to the line that became Max-Well Wheatens. Barbara Miller was her partner. No longer active in Wheatens, Mrs. Miller continues to use the name for her successful Norfolk Terrier line.

The author and Lady Patricia of Windmill (Tanjybairn ex Leprecaun's Lovely Colleen) traveled around the metropolitan New York area with Jackie Gottlieb and Ch. Stephen Dedalus of Andover, CD, ROM (Leprecaun's Jackeen Arrah ex Andover Antic of Sunset Hill). "Sweeney" had a profound influence on the breed as the sire of forty-three champions; he is truly the "breed's American patriarch" (*Terrier Type*, July 1987).

Wheatens now began to be seen more regularly in the Miscellaneous class. It was in the years 1968 to 1973 that a substantial core of breeders and exhibitors developed. In this limited gene pool, a great deal of breeding took place. We were all pretty much novices, but we shared what we knew. The more experienced owners and breeders helped the newcomers.

Some of the best known and most important currently active breeders got their start in this rather brief span of time. It only seemed long to anxious Wheaten people.

These breeders came into Wheatens from different directions but their goal was the same, to gain AKC acceptance by breeding typey, sound animals. On March 13, 1973, the board of directors of the American Kennel Club voted to accept the SCWTCA Stud Book and grant the breed full registration. Show eligibility would commence as of October 1, 1973.

That first October weekend of recognition saw the first champion finished and established the Montgomery County weekend as *the* place for Wheatens to be each October. Recognition had been achieved but full glory was yet to come.

Thus we have the pioneers. Some of these breeders and exhibitors showed terrier stamina in their pursuit of recognition for their beloved breed. They developed the breed to the stage where the Wheaten had most of its original traits, but a style and presentation that is unique.

From the foregoing history, it is apparent that the Soft Coated Wheaten Terrier owes a great deal to Maureen Holmes and the dogs she bred and exported to America. The following notes are from a

1989 interview. They do not begin to convey the dynamism of this most fascinating woman who kept the Soft Coated Wheaten Terrier from receding back into the Irish mist forever.

INTERVIEW WITH MAUREEN HOLMES

On September 7, 1989, I had the great good fortune to spend the afternoon talking with Maureen Holmes, that indomitable Irish lady to whose fabled dogs the American Wheaten traces its roots. It was just a stroke of luck that I found out that not only was she here in the United States, but also that she was in Connecticut visiting some longtime friends. A Saturday cookout was to be given in her honor by Virginia and Ray Potter.

As much as I wanted to attend the barbecue, I really wanted to speak to her in a more intimate setting. Sally Sotirovich, who knew Maureen's hosts, arranged for the two of us to visit on a Thursday afternoon. At first we had hoped to videotape or record the visit, but Mrs. Holmes was not comfortable with the high-tech world of video and so that plan was squelched.

So we went, I with a list of questions, Sally with her computer printout of all the Irish pedigrees. Despite traffic, we arrived in mid afternoon and were warmly greeted by the friendly, confident woman who had been breeding Wheatens for over forty years, a woman who inspired feelings of awe and respect and perhaps even a bit of fear. I had met her in New Jersey nearly twenty years ago. My most vivid memory is that she had one of the firmest handshakes I ever felt before or since.

On this afternoon she really looked wonderful. She certainly had aged well. Her eyes are bright blue, and they sparkle when she talks, especially about Wheatens.

The first thing she did was to show us pictures of some dogs of her breeding in Ireland and Finland. She also had a photo of a clearly Wheaten dog that came from a well-bred Kerry Blue Terrier litter and was indeed registered as such. There was some anxiety on my part, as I wasn't sure whether the questions I wanted to ask were appropriate. I really wanted to know about her background so I asked questions about how she started in Wheatens and about memorable dogs that she had bred.

She said she was given an ''Irish'' Terrier when her son was quite young which turned out to be a Wheaten. She had a Wire Fox Terrier for a while but became involved in Wheatens in the 1940s. She whelped her first Wheaten litter in 1943 and still breeds both Wheatens and Yorkies. During her lifetime, she bred and owned many Greyhounds, Salukis, Westies, Poodles, Dalmatians, Finnish Spitz and Yorkies and, of course, Wheatens. She currently owns one Wheaten and two Yorkies. She has bred more than four thousand dogs in her nearly fifty years in dogs.

Mrs. Holmes's husband, who died in 1979, worked for the Land Department. They were a team, and he shared many of her doggy activities. She says that a lot of her enthusiasm died when he did and the recent loss of her only son has taken a bit of the edge off her innate joie de vivre.

Maureen's father died when she was one year old. He was a lawyer and she admits to having inherited his methodical, orderly ways. Her mother and grandmother raised her. Her grandfather was a doctor and at his death left his wife quite well off. Maureen went to school in France and can still hold her own in conversations with French speakers she meets.

For the entire afternoon, she regaled us with stories of her experiences in the world of dogs. Some of them were hilarious, quite revealing and not meant to be in print. She judges on the continent frequently and seems to have total recall about the dogs she has seen.

She is outspoken and candid about almost everything. This is a woman who has the courage of her convictions. Even if you do not agree with her, she is so forceful in her statements and opinions that you sometimes begin to question your own judgment.

She gave us a copy of the Irish Standard. As I read it, words jumped off the page that perfectly described some of Maureen's traits: hardy, active, giving the idea of strength, spirited, good tempered, intelligent. Like every Wheaten I know, she has an excellent memory. Throughout the visit I had the feeling I was in the presence of a rare and unusual person.

The day went on and we talked and talked. She told us about her campaign to recover the Irish breeds when the Federation Cynologique Internationale decided to designate all the native breeds except the Irish Water Spaniel as having originated in England. This meant that all over Europe and South America, Wheatens would be judged by the English Standard. To Maureen, nothing worse could befall the breed. She embarked on a prolific letter-writing campaign to kennel clubs, breeders, political figures and anyone else that she thought might have some influence with FCI. Finally, she achieved her goal and Ireland got back its native breeds.

I really wanted the visit to go on and on but our hosts wanted to dine and the two unexpected guests had to break away. Even as we said our good-byes there was another story which I can't repeat here. Maureen had written an article for a British obedience magazine called *Heel*. The editor's foreword describes Maureen Holmes as a woman loved by 92 percent of the people who know her. Count me as one of them.

Mrs. Maureen Holmes during a 1989 visit to the United States.

Ch. Wildflower Stardust won Best of Breed at
all three shows on Montgomery weekend
1985. He is shown here at the Specialty
presentation with judge Barbara Keenan and
handler Maripi Woolridge.

```
                   Ch. Koop's Kilkenny of Woodbridge, ROM
              Ch. Gleanngay Holliday, ROM
                   Ch. Gleanngay's Goldilach, ROM
         Ch. Jamboree Gleanngay Gaucho
                   Ch. Abby's Postage Dhu O'Waterford, ROM
              Ch. Gleanngay's Glamoira
                   Ch. Innisfree's Annie Sullivan, ROM
    Ch. Gleanngay Gather Moon Dust
                   Ch. Raclee Express West O'Andover, CD, ROM
              Ch. Briarlyn Dandelion, ROM
                   Ch. Kenwood's Abbey O'Briarlyn
         Ch. Gleanngay Motown Moonflower
                   Ch. Abby's Postage Dhu O'Waterford, ROM
              Ch. Gleanngay Gather Moonbeams
                   Ch. Innisfree's Annie Sullivan, ROM
Ch. Wildflower Stardust
                   Leprecaun's Jackeen Arrah
              Ch. Stephen Dedalus of Andover, CD, ROM
                   Andover Antic of Sunset Hill
         Ch. Abby's Postage Dhu O'Waterford, ROM
                   Katie's Doctor Dhu Little
              Berdot's Brigette
                   Berdot's Peg O'Our Hearts
    Ch. Gleanngay Gotta Be Me
                   Gallagher of Sunset Hill
              O'Callahan of Sunset Hill
                   Mocara of Sunset Hill
         Ch. Innisfree's Annie Sullivan, ROM
                   Holmenocks Grand Coup
              Croombour Crackerjill
                   Croom Crespina
```

5

The Soft Coated Wheaten Terrier in the United States Since 1974

ONCE the Soft Coated Wheaten Terrier had been accepted as a registerable breed, new milestones were reached each year. As the number of dogs grew, new breeders and exhibitors came into the breed. At the same time, many of the people who went through the trials and tribulations of the years in the Miscellaneous class remained actively involved. They continued to show and breed with great success. The SCWTCA kept up its role as protector of the breed with its education programs. The Wheaten was still the "new kid on the block" in the terrier world. It was time to prove that this shaggy, blond terrier from Erin's isle was worthy of its place.

This chapter covers the years after 1973, but since history is a continuum some of the people and dogs discussed here could just as easily have been included in the previous chapter. They were an integral part of those early years, but their impact on the breed is of greater import in this later era.

By looking at the show records of the top winners of this period and examining their pedigrees, it will be readily apparent that a relatively small number of dogs and breeders have set the Wheaten mold in the United States. This influence will continue to be felt as the descendants of these important dogs make their own mark in Wheaten history.

AMADEN

The Amaden prefix is one of the oldest Wheaten lines still active. It belongs to Emily Holden and Carol Carlson. In Gaelic *amaden* means "fool" which is what Emily's mother called Carol and Emily when they came back from Ireland with Irish Ch. Benmul Belma.

Amaden Wheatens started with dogs from several different breeders at a time when there was not a lot of choice. In 1965 Carol Carlson purchased Ballymoor Heather (Cobalt Bourcro Ballybay ex Cornbin Tanjareen) from Natalie Maguire. Three years later, she obtained Roscommon's Uncommon of Sunset Hill (Gallagher of Sunset Hill ex Mocara of Sunset Hill) from Constance Willis.

In 1971, Emily bought Jenny Love of Addison Mews (Brenock's Kelly's Lucky Charm ex Roscommon's Uncommon of Sunset Hill) from Carol and Amaden's Katie Love (Dungarvin of Sunset Hill ex Brydie of Balitara) from Anne Elwell. Her next addition was Brydie of Balitara (Benker Belton ex Gramachrees Eivlin Aruin) also from Anne Elwell (Slievehoven).

This was the beginning of an enduring partnership. Emily and Carol imported Irish Ch. Benmul Belma in 1971. Belma (Holmenocks Hancock ex Hurley's Lass) was handled by the well-known terrier handler Peter Green and compiled an outstanding record in the Miscellaneous class. While Belma was taken out by Peter, Carol and Emily went south and west campaigning Katie Love and Amaden McBuff of Sunset Hill (O'Callahan of Sunset Hill ex Cobalt Bourtor Ballynilty) and praising the Wheaten to all who would listen.

Belma was the second Wheaten to become a champion in 1973. Carol and Emily then embarked on a breeding program that began with a mating between Jenny Love and Ch. Koop's Kilkenny of Woodridge, ROM (Ch. Abby's Postage Dhu O'Waterford, ROM, ex O'Hagan's Cindy of Ashworth.) A bitch from that mating, Ch. Amaden's Rainbows End, was bred to Ch. Templemore Marathon Man (Ch. Gleanngay Holliday, ROM, ex Ch. Gleanngay's Gwyneth) and

Roscommon's Uncommon of Sunset Hill.

Ch. Jenny Love of Addison Mews.

Binheath Pippykin
Kelly of Binheath
Binheath's Kandy
Binheath Perro Benito
Seamus of Binheath
Kilndown Macushla
Gay of Binheath
Brenock's Kelly's Lucky Charm
Holmenocks Grand Coup
Cobalt Bourcro Ballybay
Croom Crespina
Little Mermaid of the Egerluk
Holmenocks Hamish
Pride of Marretthays
Golden Moss
Ch. Jenny Love of Addison Mews
Holmenocks Grand Coup
Cobalt Bourcro Ballybay
Croom Crespina
Gallagher of Sunset Hill
Gads Hill
Katie O' Cobalt
Holmenocks Hallmark
Roscommon's Uncommon of Sunset Hill
Holmenocks Grand Coup
Cobalt Bourcro Ballybay
Croom Crespina
Mocara of Sunset Hill
Melauburn
Holmenocks Hallmark
Holmenocks Hilite

produced Ch. Amaden's Tess of Marabow who was then bred back to Holliday. Ch. Amaden's Kate of Marabow, one of the resulting bitches, was a Group winner and top producer.

Rainbow's End bred to Ch. Gleanngay Holliday, ROM, produced five champions, one of whom, Ch. Amaden's Abbey Holiday, was bred back to her sire. This mating produced Ch. Amaden's Leading Man, one of Amaden's most successful dogs.

ANDOVER

In the late 1980s, Ch. Andover Song 'n Dance Man (Ch. Gleanngay Holliday, ROM, ex Ch. Andover Hootenanny), "Harry," compiled an enviable show record. In the Wheaten world, the year revolves around the Montgomery County Kennel Club weekend and the SCWTCA annual Specialty. In 1989 Harry was Best of Breed at the Specialty, capping a year in which he won the Terrier Group at the Westminster Kennel Club show under judge William Bergum. That was the first time a Wheaten ever placed in the Group at the Garden, and winning it was truly a milestone for the breed.

Harry won his first Specialty show in 1986 at the SCWTC of Southern California under breeder-judge Gay Sherman. He won the SCWTCA Roving Speciality in 1986 and the National Specialty in 1987 and 1988. In 1988 he also won Specialty shows in Denver, Chicago and southern California.

In addition to winning the Group at Westminster, Harry was BB at the June 1989 Specialty held by the SCWTC of Metropolitan New York in Greenwich, Connecticut, and the SCWTCA Roving in New Haven, Connecticut. He has won five all-breed Best in Show awards as of this writing.

A dog like Harry may come along once in a lifetime, but his appearance is not a fluke. Jackie Gottlieb and her daughter, Cindy Vogels, have spent more than twenty years developing the Andover strain by careful, planned breedings.

The first Wheaten in the Gottlieb household was "Maggie," officially known as Andover Antic of Sunset Hill (Cobalt Bourcro Ballybay ex Katie O'Cobalt). She was bought as a pet and shared the Gottlieb's gracious Andover Road home in Rockville Centre, New York, until the family moved to Colorado where she continued to "rule the roost" until her death in 1983.

Maggie was bred to Leprecaun's Jackeen Arrah in 1970. The

Ch. Andover Song 'n Dance Man, ROM, owned by Cindy Vogels, winning the Terrier Group at the Westminster Kennel Club show in 1989 under judge William Bergum. William Rockefeller is the Trophy presenter. Sally George is the handler. "Harry" has won five all-breed Bests in Show and a host of Specialty Bests.

John Ashbey

Ch. Glenworth Andover Answer, ROM, produced more champions than any other Wheaten bitch through 1989. *Wayne Cott*

resulting litter was named after characters from James Joyce's book *Portrait of the Artist as a Young Man*. Two dogs from that litter were basic to the Andover line, Ch. Stephen Dedalus of Andover ("Sweeney") and Cissy Caffrey of Andover. Cissy was sold to Karen Worth and when bred to Harrigan of Hopping Brook (Brenock's Kelly's Lucky Charm ex Mocara of Sunset Hill), she produced Ch. Glenworth Andover Answer, ROM, the Gottlieb's top producing bitch, and Ch. Glenworth's Country Squire, ROM, who remained at Glenworth.

Squire was bred to Ruth Stein's bitch Am./Ber. Ch. Raclee's Serendipity (Ch. Stephen Dedalus of Andover, CD, ROM, ex Leprecaun's Golden Heather). One of the puppies from that litter was Ch. Raclee Express West O'Andover, CD, ROM. "Ryan" was Cindy's house dog when he was not on the show circuit with a professional handler. Ryan and Answer form the basis for the current Andover line.

Ryan's show record includes winning the first SCWTCA Specialty in 1975 and the first SCWTCA Roving Specialty in 1976. He is one of the breed's leading sires with over eighty-four champion get. Ryan was bred to Ch. Andover Fair Dinkum Ad Lib (Honeywoods Cobby Obby ex Ch. Andover Fair Dinkum Chanty) and produced Ch. Andover Hootenanny who in turn produced "Harry," the top winning Wheaten in the history of the breed whose contributions to the breed and to Andover as a sire continue as this book goes to press.

WATERFORD

Marjorie and Dan Shoemaker bought their first Wheaten, Glocca Morra's Ian Harrigan, CDX (Callahan of Sunset Hill ex Long Ridge Eileen Aroon) in 1970. Ch. Cloverlane's Connaught CD (Gramachree's Dermod O'Derry ex Thistledown of the Egerluk) and Gilchrist's Dena of Waterford (Dungarvin of Sunset Hill ex Gilchrist Gal O'Slievehoven) were soon added to the Shoemakers' new "Waterford" household. Marjorie's immediate attraction to Ch. Abby's Postage Dhu O'Waterford, ROM (Ch. Stephen Dedalus of Andover, CD, ROM, ex Berdot's Brigette) resulted in the addition of a fourth and truly important Wheaten to the clan.

Postage Dhu, whose call name was "Casey," became the first champion in the breed in October 1973 during the first weekend of full recognition. Basing their breeding program on these four dogs has led the Shoemakers through twenty years of success in the breed. Casey

Ch. Raclee Express West O'Andover, CD, ROM, owned by Cynthia Gottlieb. "Ryan" was a leading sire, having produced eighty-four champions through 1987.
William Gilbert

Ch. Abby's Postage Dhu O'Waterford, ROM, the breed's first champion, owned by Marjorie Shoemaker.   *William Gilbert*

Binheath Perro Benito
Brenock's Kelly's Lucky Charm
Little Mermaid of the Egerluk
Harrigan of Hopping Brook
Cobalt Bourcro Ballybay
Mocara of Sunset Hill
Holmenocks Hallmark
Ch. Glenworth's Country Squire, ROM
Gramachree's Minute Man, CDX
Leprecaun's Jackeen Arrah
Holmenocks Hispanola
Cissy Caffrey of Andover
Cobalt Bourcro Ballybay
Andover Antic of Sunset Hill
Katie O'Cobalt
Ch. Raclee Express West O'Andover, CD, ROM
Gramachree's Minute Man, CDX
Leprecaun's Jackeen Arrah
Holmenocks Hispanola
Ch. Stephen Dedalus of Andover, CD, ROM
Cobalt Bourcro Ballybay
Andover Antic of Sunset Hill
Katie O'Cobalt
Ch. Raclee's Serendipity
Cobalt Bourcro Ballybay
Tanjybairn
Cornbin Tanjareen
Leprecaun's Golden Heather
Gramachree's Minute Man, CDX
Mistress Maggie of Leprecaun
Holmenocks Hispanola

Gads Hill
Gramachree's Minute Man, CDX
Holmenocks Gramachree, CD
Leprecaun's Jackeen Arrah
Holmenocks Hackney
Holmenocks Hispanola
Holmenocks Henrietta
Ch. Stephen Dedalus of Andover, CD, ROM
Holmenocks Grand Coup
Cobalt Bourcro Ballybay
Croom Crespina
Andover Antic of Sunset Hill
Gads Hill
Kate O'Cobalt
Holmenocks Hallmark
Ch. Abby's Postage Dhu O'Waterford, ROM
Gramachree's Minute Man, CDX
Gramachree's Roderick Dhu, CD
Faraderry Fairy, CDX
Katie's Doctor Dhu Little
Cobalt Bourcro Ballybay
Sunset Hills Kilkenny Kate
Katie O'Cobalt
Berdot's Brigette
Gramachree's Minute Man, CDX
Gramachree's Deoch An Dorais
Faraderry Fairy, CDX
Berdot's Peg O'Our Hearts
Grants Hill Downeaster
Grants Hill Ocean Melody
Holmenocks Hailsworth

appears in the pedigrees of a majority of the champions finished between 1975 and 1986.

Marjorie also showed Ch. Koop's Kilkenny of Woodridge, ROM (Ch. Abby's Postage Dhu O'Waterford, ROM, ex O'Hagan's Cindy of Ashworth) to his title. He stayed at Waterford for a time and was used frequently at stud. One of his best known offspring is Ch. Gleanngay Holliday, ROM.

Another breeder who began with Waterford stock was Beverly Trapani (Greentree). She and her husband, Tom, purchased Ch. Waterford Red Rose, ROM (Ch. Briarlyn Dandelion, ROM, ex Ch. Cloverlane's Connaught, CD) from the Shoemakers in 1977. In a breeding to Ch. Gleanngay Holliday, ROM, Rose produced Ch. Greentree Man O'Waterford, ROM, who has sired at least twenty-eight champions.

Waterford dogs also helped Nona Harwell (Harwelden) to get started in Wheatens. Nona obtained Ch. Lejerdell's Cut Crystal, a Casey daughter out of Ch. Kate Dedalus of Forest Glen. Cut Crystal was twice bred back to her sire. The progeny included Ch. Waterford Harwelden's Deuce and Ch. Waterford Harwelden Blast.

Obviously, the major Waterford influence came through Casey, who figures in so many lines. Casey was always owner-handled. He was the first BOB and the first Wheaten champion. He led all terrier sires in 1975 and 1976 in numbers of champions sired. He died in 1984 at age twelve, leaving an enduring mark on the breed.

GLEANNGAY

Gay Sherman credits Charlie Arnold and Anne Elwell for locating Jean Free, who had a litter with two promising bitches. The dog Gay chose was to become one of the outstanding early bitches in the breed, Ch. Innisfree's Annie Sullivan, ROM (O'Callahan of Sunset Hill ex Croombour Crackerjill).

Annie produced twenty champions; five became top producers, and they in turn have produced outstanding progeny. Annie's first litter was sired by Ch. Stephen Dedalus of Andover, CD, ROM (''Sweeney''), the second and fourth by Postage Dhu, the third by Ch. Gleanngay's Gingerbread Man who was out of the Sweeney litter and the fifth by Ch. Koop's Kilkenny of Woodbridge, ROM, a Casey son.

Annie was the third Wheaten to become a champion and the first to win an all-breed Best in Show. This historic milestone came on St. Patrick's day in 1974 at the Tidewater Kennel Club. While Annie's

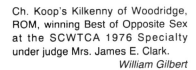

Ch. Innisfree's Annie Sullivan, ROM (O'Callahan of Sunset Hill ex Croombour Crackerjill) represents a major milestone in the history of the Soft Coated Wheaten Terrier. She is shown here being awarded Best in Show at the Tidewater Kennel Club under judge Jane G. Kay; it was the first BIS for the breed and came, appropriately, on St. Patrick's Day, 1974. Annie, in addition to being a strong winner, was a noted producer. Owned by Gay Sherman, she was shown in the ring by Roberta Campbell. *Lucas*

Ch. Koop's Kilkenny of Woodridge, ROM, winning Best of Opposite Sex at the SCWTCA 1976 Specialty under judge Mrs. James E. Clark.
William Gilbert

show record was impressive, it was in the whelping box that her qualities really shone through. Her true terrier temperament, spirit and structure showed up in her offspring. Gay recognized that Annie's standaway coat was her one serious fault. In an article in *Benchmarks*, Gay maintained that Annie won in spite of her coat.

By judicious breeding to dogs with good coats, Gay was able to overcome the coat problem. Five of the puppies from the Sweeney litter went to show homes and finished their titles. Ch. Gleanngay's Ginger Peach was an important bitch for Jack and Marcia Cohan's Erinmore line. Ch. Gleanngay's Gibrien of Gael is the grandsire of Can., Am. Ch. Ballynacally's Eden Princess, bred and owned by Bryan and Mary Lynne Reynolds.

Gay considered it a great stroke of luck when she got Ch. Gleanngay's Goldilach back from her previous owner. "Taffy" was bred to Ch. Koop's Kilkenny of Woodbridge, ROM, and produced Ch. Gleanngay Holliday, ROM, whose call name was "Doc." Here was a dog to be reckoned with, a watershed dog, deservedly joining the ranks of other significant sires, Stephen Dedalus, Postage Dhu and his own sire, Koop's Kilkenny, all of whom appear in his pedigree at least once.

Doc's contribution to the breed is unquestioned. To quote Marjorie Shoemaker in a tribute to Annie Sullivan in the January 1987 *Terrier Type*, "Like his father Brandy, Doc is an extreme dog, and that very extreme-ness had added to the elegance, grace and outline of our breed. . . . As I see it, the 'Good Doctor' has the cure for the common Wheaten."

Another important dog to Gleanngay was Ch. Briarlyn Dandelion, ROM (Ch. Raclee Express West O'Andover, CD, ROM, ex Ch. Kenwood's Abbey O'Briarlyn). Dandy was used on Ch. Gleanngay Gather Moonbeams, a Casey-Annie daughter, and Can., Am. Ch. Gleanngay Moon Marigold (Gay leased her for two litters), a Doc-Moonbeam daughter. Gay named these "Motown" litters after Dandy's hometown of Detroit.

Waterford's Jennifer Juniper, "Juney," (Ch. Abby's Postage Dhu O'Waterford, ROM, ex Ch Cloverlane's Connaught, CD) was the only bitch from another breeder that Gay added to her breeding program since she bought Annie Sullivan. Juney produced Ch. Gleanngay Shenanigans when bred to Ch. Gleanngay Henry Buttons. Shenanigans went to Everett and Frederica Keller's Ballyhoo Kennels.

Over the years, dogs with the Gleanngay name have provided foundation stock to other breeders, among them Janet Turner (Wildflower) and Candy Way (Bantry Bay). In addition to Ballyhoo, the

94

Ch. Gleanngay Holliday, ROM, with handler Penny Belviso.

Leprecaun's Jackeen Arrah
Ch. Stephen Dedalus of Andover, CD, ROM
Andover Antic of Sunset Hill
Ch. Abby's Postage Dhu O'Waterford, ROM
Katie's Doctor Dhu Little
Berdot's Brigette
Berdot's Peg O'Our Hearts
Ch. Koop's Kilkenny of Woodridge, ROM
Bennekerry Beechnut
Berdot's Irish Whiskey
Berdot's Peg O'Our Hearts
O'Hagan's Cindy of Ashworth
Grants Hill Lumberjack
Sagecrest's Shamrock,CDX
Berdot's Irish Mist, CD
Ch. Gleanngay Holliday, ROM
Gramachree's Minute Man, CDX
Leprecaun's Jackeen Arrah
Holmenocks Hispanola
Ch. Stephen Dedalus of Andover, CD, ROM
Cobalt Bourcro Ballybay
Andover Antic of Sunset Hill
Katie O'Cobalt
Ch. Gleanngay's Goldilach, ROM
Gallagher of Sunset Hill
O'Callahan of Sunset Hill
Mocara of Sunset Hill
Ch. Innisfree's Annie Sullivan, ROM
Holmenocks Grand Coup
Croombour Crackerjill
Croom Crespina

West Coast Wheaten ranks were enhanced by the addition of Ch. Gleanngay's Grainnie, a Casey-Annie daughter who went to Jackie Luckenbaugh (Everwil) and Ch. Gleanngay Full Moon Fan Dance (Ch. Gleanngay Motown Moondance ex Can., Am. Ch. Gleanngay Moon Marigold, Can. CD, ROM) owned by Susan Strange (Carlinayer).

The Casey-Annie breeding produced other bitches that became foundation dams for Jocelyn Slatin (Jamboree) and Frank Maselli (Templemore). Ch. Gleanngay's Glamoira went to Jamboree in Chicago and Ch. Gleanngay's Gwyneth to Templemore in Massachusetts.

One of the Dandy-Moonbeam daughters, Ch. Gleanngay Motown Moonflower, was sold to Candace Little as a foundation bitch for her Candace line. Another relative newcomer using Gleanngay stock is McGillicauddy Wheatens who started with Ch. Gleanngay Holy Spirit (Ch. Gleanngay Motown Mannequin ex Ch. Gleanngay Holy Hannah).

Gay and her Gleanngay Wheatens moved from Williamstown, Massachusetts, to Sellersville, Pennsylvania, to Santa Fe, New Mexico. She has never lost sight of her goals as a breeder. The Gleanngay name is firmly entrenched in Wheaten history. If Gay never breeds another dog—heaven forbid—her accomplishments will stand as an enduring model to those who follow.

As a digression, it is interesting to note how the four lines— Amaden, Andover, Waterford and Gleanngay—have become intertwined over the years. There was a time when dogs were not considered potential sires because of who owned them. At various points in time, breeders were in opposite camps for a number of reasons. It is a credit to the foresight and honesty of these breeders that the progress of the breed became the most important goal.

In the July 1987 issue of *Terrier Type*, Gay Sherman, in discussing Wheaten progress, said, ". . . this growth is directly attributable to the close personal relationships of a small, dedicated few who put the producing of quality Wheaten Terriers above all other aspects of the dog game." These, then, are the breeders who have set the Wheaten mold. Their contribution to the breed's development is unquestioned.

These four lines have shaped today's Wheaten. Since 1975, nearly all the top producers, Specialty winners and ROM dogs go back to one or more of these main branches of the Wheaten family tree. In looking at some of the lines that emanate from them, a clear picture

Ch. Gleanngay Gather Moon Dust (Ch. Gleanngay Jamboree Gaucho ex Ch. Gleanngay Motown Moonflower) winning Best of Breed at Westchester in 1983. He is handled by Gay Sherman.

William Gilbert

Ch. Gleanngay Gotta Be Me (Ch. Abby's Postage Dhu O'Waterford ex Ch. Innisfree's Annie Sullivan, ROM) was Janet Turner's foundation bitch for the Wildflower line. *William Gilbert*

develops of the impact a few dogs have made on the course of Wheaten history.

LEGENDERRY

Jack and Audrey Weintraub bought their first Wheaten in 1969, Ch. Tammara of Balitara, CD (Benker Belton ex Gramachrees Eivlin Aruin). "Deirdre" was the matriarch of the Legenderry line. She was bred to Leprecaun's Golden Elf in 1970 and Audrey kept a bitch, Legenderry's Ainlee, CD, ROM. In 1971 a breeding between Deirdre and Ch. Stephen Dedalus of Andover, CD, ROM, produced Legenderry's Dervorgael and Legenderry's Iollann the Fair, ROM. These two bitches were the foundations for Nina Cassel's Tain Wheatens and Sue and Harvey Goldberg's Shandalee line.

Ainlee produced thirteen champion get between 1973 and 1982, earning her a place in the ROM record book as a top producing Wheaten bitch. Ainlee was bred to Sweeney six different times and twelve of her champion get were sired by him.

In addition to Tain and Shandalee, Legenderry progeny were basic to other lines. Ch. Legenderry's Februa was sold to Sherry Yanow of Crackerjack Wheatens. Februa produced seven champions in four different breedings. She was bred to Ch. Mellickway Crackerjack, ROM, Ch. Raclee Express West O'Andover, CD, ROM, Ch. Crackerjacks Hallmark, ROM, and Ch. Gleanngay Holliday, ROM.

Ch. Legenderry Tailltu, ROM, went to Ed McParlan of Kenwood Wheatens. In very limited breeding, she produced eleven champions including two top producers, Ch. Kenwood Whitecrest MacBrody and Ch. Felicity Cara of Kenwood.

Two other Sweeney-Ainlee bitches produced fifteen champions: Ch. Legenderry's Ardan, CD, and Ch. Legenderry's Babe in the Woods. Ardan was owned by Barryglen Wheatens (Dorothy Barry), another West Coast breeder. The Weintraubs still breed an occasional litter but no longer show their dogs extensively.

TAIN

Nina Cassel started in Wheatens with Dougal of Balitara, a littermate to Ch. Tammara of Balitara, CD. She campaigned "Vic" in the Miscellaneous classes where she met Audrey Weintraub, from

Ch. Tammara of Balitara, CD. "Deirdre" was the foundation bitch for Audrey and Jack Weintraub's Legenderry line.   *John Ashbey*

Ch. Hogan of Hopping Brook, sire of seventeen champions, eleven of whom were out of Legenderry's Iollann the Fair, Sue and Harvey Goldberg's foundation bitch for their Shandalee line.

Holmenocks Handley	Binheath Pippykin
Holmenocks Hackney	Kelly of Binheath
Holmenocks Homespun	Binheath's Kandy
Holmenocks Hancock	Binheath Perro Benito
Holmenocks Grand Coup	Seamus of Binheath
Holmenocks Henrietta	Kilndown Macushla
Holmenocks Hermella	Gay of Binheath
Benker Belton	Brenock's Kelly's Lucky Charm
Holmenocks Hartigan	Holmenocks Grand Coup
Holmenocks Grand Coup	Cobalt Bourcro Ballybay
Holmenocks Herald	Croom Crespina
Hurley's Lass	Little Mermaid of the Egerluk
Mullinahone Boy	Holmenocks Hamish
Mullinahone Lass	Pride of Marretthays
Lady Fair	Golden Moss
Ch. Tammara of Balitara, CD	Ch. Hogan of Hopping Brook, ROM
Melauburn	Holmenocks Hartigan
Gads Hill	Holmenocks Grand Coup
Holmenocks Herald	Holmenocks Herald
Gramachree's Minute Man, CDX	Cobalt Bourcro Ballybay
Holmenocks Hartigan	Holmenocks Hartigan
Holmenocks Gramachree, CD	Croom Crespina
Griselda	Pudsy
Gramachree's Evilin Aruin	Mocara of Sunset Hill
Melauburn	Holmenocks Handley
Garfield Hiball	Melauburn
Griselda	Holmenocks Hunch
Faraderry Fairy, CDX	Holmenocks Hallmark
Melauburn	Holmenocks Kismi Hardy
Holmenocks Halcyon	Holmenocks Hilite
Holmenocks Hilite	Handsome Hallmark of Holmenocks

99

whom she bought Legenderry's Dervorgael ("Teelin'"), a Sweeney-Deirdre daughter. For her first letter, Teelin' was bred to Shamrock O'Perro of Brandy Keg (Binheath Perro Benito ex Little Mermaid of the Egerluk).

From this first mating came two males, Ch. Tain's Sir Nigel Loring and Ch. Tain's Brigadier Gerard, CD. The latter was a foundation male in Virginia Potter's Chermar Kennels. Sir Nigel was the patriarch of Jason Wheatens owned by Jerry Stifelman and Ian McDermott.

Teelin' was bred to Postage Dhu in 1976 and three champions resulted: Ch. Tains Pride of Chermar went to Virginia Potter, Ch. Tains Show Stopper was sold to John King and Thomas Mills of Brawic Wheatens (later to Wavehill Wheatens) and Nina kept Ch. Tains Stand Up and Cheer.

Nina has not bred extensively but she is still involved. The dogs she has bred have been well placed to carry on the Tain line.

SHANDALEE

Sue and Harvey Goldberg bought their first Wheaten from the Weintraubs in 1972. Legenderry's Iollann the Fair, ROM (Ch. Stephen Dedalus of Andover ex Ch. Tammara of Balitara, CD), was the foundation bitch for the Shandalee line. In 1976, Sue got another Legenderry bitch, Ch. Legenderry Shandalee Sho-Off, from a Sweeney-Ainlee breeding.

Sue used Hogan of Hopping Brook, ROM (Brenock's Kelly's Lucky Charm ex Mocara of Sunset Hill), with both Iollann and Sho-Off. He was bred by Constance Willis, and Sue eventually purchased him. Her most successful winners were based on these breedings. Iollann's twelve champion get were sired by Hogan.

Over the years Sue has made great contributions to the welfare of the breed. In addition to exhibiting almost every weekend she makes it a point to educate potential owners about the joys and the pitfalls of Wheaten ownership.

LONTREE

This kennel name belongs to Joy Laylon of Williamsport, Pennsylvania. Joy has been involved in Wheatens since 1971. She started

Ch. Lontree's Borstal Boy winning Best in Show under judge Dr. H. Lee Huggins at Alamance Kennel Club in 1980. This was the first Best in Show for a Wheaten since Ch. Innisfree's Annie Sullivan won the breed's first top prize at the Tidewater Kennel Club on March 17, 1974.

Graham photo by Bonnie

Ch. Wildflower Snapdragon, ROM, was a top producer of Group and Specialty winners as well as being a Specialty winner himself. Here he takes Best of Breed at the 1984 Metro (New York) Specialty under judge Ken McDermott. Penny Belviso, handler, Rubin Kaplan, Specialty Chairman, presenting trophy.

William Gilbert

101

out with Cloverlane's Clonmacnois ("Lonnie"), a sister to Marjorie Shoemaker's Cloverlane's Connaught (Gramachree's Dermod O'Derry ex Thistledown of the Egerluk), as her foundation bitch. A breeding to her littermate, Cloverlane's Cavan, resulted in Ch. Lontree's Killarney Kip, Lontree's first champion. Lonnie was next bred to Abby's Postage Dhu and produced three champions, one of whom was Ch. Lontree's Lil Dhu Drop, ROM.

Joy then added another bitch from a Casey-Dena breeding, Ch. Waterford Lontree Lace, ROM ("Lacy"), to her kennel. These two top producing bitches were the foundations of the Lontree line. Lontree dogs have scored notable successes in the ring and in the whelping box.

One of the most successful Lontree dogs was Am., Can. Ch. Lontree's Borstal Boy, sired by Ch. Raclee Express West O'Andover, CD, ROM, out of Lacy. In 1980, he was the first Wheaten since Ch. Innisfree's Annie Sullivan to win an all-breed Best in Show. He was also the first Wheaten to win more than one Best in Show.

Another big winner was Ch. Lontree's Star Waggin, ROM, who was BOB at the National Specialty in 1984. He placed in numerous groups and won two other Specialty shows. Joy keeps rather tightly to Lontree in her breeding program but does not hesitate to use dogs from other lines.

BRENMOOR

Lontree dogs also influenced other lines. Brenmoor is the kennel name chosen by Bill Behan and Gary Vlachos when they started in Wheatens. Their foundation bitch was Am., Can. Ch. Harwelden's Miss Dub-Lyn, ROM (Ch. Briarlyn Dandelion, ROM, Ch. Harwelden's Arabesque, ROM).

Gary and Bill have bred her and Borstal Boy selectively and both are top producers. A grandson, Ch. Brenmoor's Spark Plug, is also a multiple Best in Show and Specialty winner. Although they are relative newcomers, these partners have made a substantial impact on the breed.

WILDFLOWER

Janet Turner's first Wheaten was purchased as a pet. Janet had no intention of getting into dogs at that time but as fate would have it, she

Ch. Brenmoor's Spark Plug (Ch. Bantry Bay Gleanngay Kashmir ex Ch. Brenmoor's Double Kylemore) went Best in Show at Butler County Kennel Club in September 1988 under judge Eleanor Evers, handled by Alison Corn. This was his second top award.

Am., Can. Ch. Harwelden's Miss Dub-Lyn, foundation bitch for Brenmoor Wheatens, shown with sweepstakes judge Dan Kiedrowski, the publisher of *Terrier Type* magazine.

John Ashbey

came upon an AKC match show, entered, won and was hooked. Actually, Janet had had contact with dogs and shows as a young girl, so she recognized that her pet was not really top quality.

As a new subscriber to *Benchmarks*, she read the ads and decided that the Gleanngay type was what she wanted. She bought Ch. Gleanngay's Gotta Be Me ("Lolly") (Ch. Abby's Postage Dhu O'Waterford, ROM, ex Ch. Innisfree's Annie Sullivan, ROM), and eventually Lolly was bred to Ch. Briarlyn Dandelion, ROM. From this mating came the 1980 National Specialty Winner, Ch. Wildflower Woodbalm, ROM, and Ch. Wildflower Black Eyed Susan, ROM.

Susan was bred to Doc to improve head and topline. From this breeding came Ch. Wildflower Snapdragon, ROM, who produced Group and Specialty winners in addition to being a Specialty winner himself.

Wildflower dogs provided foundation stock for Wavehill Wheatens (John King and Tom Mills) and Harbour Hill (Susan and Steve Sakauye). In 1985, Ch. Wildflower Stardust won all three of the shows on Montgomery County weekend and then won the National Specialty in 1986.

One cannot mention Wildflower without also thinking of Julian Turner, who died in 1986. He was a most gentle and generous man with a wry sense of humor. He always said his major job with the dogs was to love them. The Wheaten world owes a great deal to this wonderful person who gave Janet the opportunity to pursue her goals in breeding Wheatens.

BUTTERGLOW

Alice Papaliolios obtained Lady Gregory of Long Ridge (Grants Hill Yankee Trader ex Binheath Cushlamacree) in 1971. That same year she purchased Ch. Duffy Muldoon (O'Callahan of Sunset Hill ex Sweet Molly Malone). These two formed the Butterglow foundation.

Alice has bred many champions and top producers. In 1976, Ch. Butterglow's Dream Weaver, owned by Nancy and Tamara Tolan, was Best of Breed at the National Specialty. Weaver was the first and only bitch to win the National Specialty. (Bitches have won the top spot at roving and local club Specialties on a number of occasions.)

Ch. Wildflower Woodbalm, owned by Tom Mills and John King, winning Best of Breed at Montgomery County under judge John Marvin in 1980. Everett Keller is also pictured.

John Ashbey

Ch. Briarlyn Dandelion, ROM, shown winning his fourth national Specialty in October 1978. The owner is Lynn Penniman, the judge Annemarie Moore.

John Ashbey

105

BRIARLYN

Lynn Penniman started her Briarlyn line with two bitches, Ch. Raclee Miss Meg O'Briarlyn, a Sweeney daughter out of Ruth Stein's Leprecaun's Golden Heather (Tanjybairn ex Leprecaun's Mistress Maggie) and Ch. Kenwood's Abbey O'Briarlyn (Ch. Glenworth's Country Squire, ROM, ex Ch. Legenderry's Tailltu, ROM) bred by Ed McParlan. In 1976, Abbey was bred to Ch. Raclee Express West O'Andover, CD, ROM.

Ch. Briarlyn Dandelion, ROM, came from that litter. Dandy made a spectacular debut by winning Best of Breed at the SCWTCA roving Specialty in June 1977 from the classes. He also was Best in Sweepstakes at the same Specialty show.

In October that year he won the National Specialty. In 1988 he won both the roving and the National Specialties, a total of four consecutive SCWTCA Specialty shows.

Dandy was another significant sire in the breed. Lynn bred many champions but Dandy was the best known. He was widely used at stud before his accidental death in 1981. He sired fifty-five champions. Nearly half of his sons and daughters were top producers themselves. One can only wonder what his impact would have been had he achieved a normal lifespan.

GLENWORTH

For longtime Wheaten fanciers, the name Glenworth immediately brings to mind Ch. Glenworth's Country Squire, ROM. (Harrigan of Hopping Brook ex Cissy Caffrey of Andover). "Murphy" was one of those special dogs that placed his stamp on his offspring. He was of moderate size and had a superb coat with excellent color which he passed on to this progeny.

Murphy was bred and owned by Ed and Karen Worth. His dam was a littermate to Sweeney. The Worths' place in Wheaten history was secured by the outstanding records compiled by Murphy and Ch. Glenworth Andover Answer, ROM. Both had the same sire and dam but they were from two different litters. Each had twenty-six champion get and Answer was the top producing bitch in the breed as of 1987.

Ch. Glenworth's Country Squire, ROM, bred and owned by Ed and Karen Worth, sired twenty-six champions, many of whom were also top producers.

Ch. Bantry Bay Gleanngay Kashmir was Best in Show at Huntington Kennel Club under judge Mrs. George Wanner. Handler, Penny Belviso. *Alverson*

Kelly of Binheath
Binheath Perro Benito
Kilndown Macushla
Brenock's Kelly's Lucky Charm
Cobalt Bourcro Ballybay
Little Mermaid of the Egerluk
Pride of Marretthays
Harrigan of Hopping Brook
Holmenocks Grand Coup
Cobalt Bourcro Ballybay
Croom Crespina
Mocara of Sunset Hill
Melauburn
Holmenocks Hallmark
Holmenocks Hilite
Ch. Glenworth's Country Squire, ROM
Gads Hill
Gramachree's Minute Man, CDX
Holmenocks Gramachree, CD
Leprecaun's Jackeen Arrah
Holmenocks Hackney
Holmenocks Hispanola
Holmenocks Henrietta
Cissy Caffrey of Andover
Holmenocks Grand Coup
Cobalt Bourcro Ballybay
Croom Crespina
Andover Antic of Sunset Hill
Gads Hill
Katie O'Cobalt
Holmenocks Hallmark

Ch. Koop's Kilkenny of Woodridge, ROM
Ch. Gleanngay Holliday, ROM
Ch. Gleanngay's Goldilach, ROM
Ch. Jamboree Gleanngay Gaucho
Ch. Abby's Postage Dhu O'Waterford, ROM
Ch. Gleanngay's Glamoira
Ch. Innisfree's Annie Sullivan, ROM
Ch. Gleanngay Gather Moon Dust
Ch. Raclee Express West O'Andover, CD, ROM
Ch. Briarlyn Dandelion, ROM
Ch. Kenwood's Abbey O'Briarlyn
Ch. Gleanngay Motown Moonflower
Ch. Abby's Postage Dhu O'Waterford, ROM
Ch. Gleanngay Gather Moonbeams
Ch. Innisfree's Annie Sullivan, ROM
Ch. Bantry Bay Gleanngay Kashmir
Ch. Abby's Postage Dhu O'Waterford, ROM
Ch. Koop's Kilkenny of Woodridge, ROM
O'Hagan's Cindy of Ashworth
Ch. Gleanngay Holliday, ROM
Ch. Stephen Dedalus of Andover, CD, ROM
Ch. Gleanngay's Goldilach, ROM
Ch. Innisfree's Annie Sullivan, ROM
Ch. Gleanngay Holly Berry
Ch. Koop's Kilkenny of Woodridge, ROM
Ch. Gleanngay Henrybuttons
Ch. Gleanngay's Goldilach, ROM
Ch. Gleanngay She's the Berries
Ch. Abby's Postage Dhu O'Waterford, ROM
Ch. Waterford Jennifer Juniper
Ch. Cloverlane's Connaught, CD

GLENKERRY

In the early years, Wheaten activity was concentrated in New York, New Jersey and Pennsylvania. Mary Pickford was one of the early Midwest breeders and chose the name Glenkerry (sometimes spelled Glenkerree) for her line.

Anne Elwell sent Slievehoven Western Traveler (Brencock's Kelly's Lucky Charm ex Toby Mug of Sunset Hill) to Betsy Finley, who lived in Minnesota. Betsy transferred the bitch to Mary Pickford in 1971. The Finleys owned Ch. Sweeney of Sunset Hill (O'Callahan of Sunset Hill ex Cobalt Bourtor Ballynilty). In 1974 he became the first Wheaten to win a Terrier Group.

Mary bred Western Traveler to Sweeney of Sunset Hill and produced Can., Am. Ch. Glenkerry the Phantom, CD, Can. CD, who became the foundation bitch for Linda Wolters' Elfinstone line.

Another line that started with Glenkerry stock was Helen Moreland's Kuhullen line. Helen Moreland also lives in Minnesota. Her first two Wheatens were Elfinstone Kelly O'Casey (Ch. Amaden's Bendacht ex Ch. Glenkerry the Phantom CD) who came from Linda Wolters and Ch. Glenkerrees Danny Boy (Sunset Hills Dingle Drummer ex Slievehoven Western Traveler) from Mary Pickford.

Helen's breeding led the Kuhullen name to join with Ed McParlan's Kenwood and Nina Kostraba's Rogue line. Ch. Kenwood's Kuhullen Kathleen (Ch. Briarlyn Dandelion, ROM, ex Ch. Kenwood's Queen Mab) and Ch. Rogue's Kuhullen Roberta (Ch. Winquest Revelation, ROM, ex Ch. Kenwoods Fann O'Nichol) are two examples. Kuhullen dogs have also gone to Canada and some have titles from both countries.

Ch. Glenkerry's Brandon Hill sired Ch. Bomier's Tammy of County Cork out of Kirshbaum's Kreema. Tammy was the dam of Ch. Bomier's Mr. McBo, a Casey son who sired seven champions.

Mary is still breeding on a limited basis. She recently obtained a bitch who is a granddaughter of Int. Ch. Newkilber the Quiet Man, one of Europe's outstanding Wheatens.

RIVERRUN

Ken and Donna Henseler raised Basset Hounds before they discovered Wheatens. They live in Yankton, South Dakota. Their first dog, Berdot's Toby Lad, was a littermate to Berdot's Brigette, dam of

108

Ch. Abby's Postage Dhu O'Waterford, ROM. They had read about the beautiful soft, silky coat and were surprised to get a puppy with a somewhat wiry coat that had no waves and did not flow. (In time, Toby's coat developed into what was then called the "Irish" coat to distinguish it from the fuller "American" coat.)

Later Berdot's Sabrina Fair (Katie's Doctor Dhu Little ex Amy's Wearin' the Green) joined the Henselers. A daughter of a Toby-Sabrina mating, Riverrun Brighid, was bred to a Stephen Dedalus son out of Sunset Hills Eleanor of Lothlorien, Lothlorien's Riverrun Strider. The mating produced a bitch, Ch. Riverrun Qlee who was the dam of Ch. Caleycrest's Amazin' Mazie, ROM, by Ch. Kuhullen's Padraeic O'Casey.

Maizie produced Ch. Windsong's I Am Music, a Specialty winner. His sire was Ch. Gleanngay Motown Mannequin. He was bred and owned by Suzanne Brown, another Midwestern breeder. Another top winner out of the Riverrun line was Ch. Mist O'Morn Riverrun Riff (Can., Am. Ch. Marima's Classical Jazz, ROM, ex Riverrun Maggie O'Cranberry, ROM.)

Even though the Henselers are geographically isolated from most Wheaten activity, their Riverrun dogs have been placed with and co-owned by others who can and do show them. It is by this avenue that Riverrun has influenced the breed.

CRACKERJACK

Another Midwestern breeder, Sherry Yanow, bred and owned some top-winning dogs during the time she and her husband, Glen, were active in Wheatens. In bitches, Sherry started out with Ch. Mt. Mellick's Devon Cream (Ch. Stephen Dedalus of Andover, CD, ROM ex Lady Patricia of Windmill) and Ch. Legenderry's Februa by Stephen Dedalus out of Tammara of Balitara, CD.

In dogs, she owned Ch. Mellickway Crackerjack, ROM ("Rory"), out of a repeat of the Devon Cream breeding done by the author. Rory was the youngest Wheaten to finish his championship. He did so at six and one-half months during the 1974 Montgomery County weekend. He placed in the Terrier Group at the International Kennel Club of Chicago in 1975. He sired twenty-one champions.

His son out of Ch. Lady Colleen of Forest Glen, ROM, Ch. Crackerjacks Hallmark, ROM ("Robin"), had an outstanding show career and produced twenty-five champions. Rory was co-owned by

Mary Lou Lafler whose Marima line has been so successful with the BIS-winning dogs, Ch. Marima's Classical Jazz, ROM (Ch. Briarlyn Kris Kringle ex Marima's Apple Brandee) and Ch. Marima's Easy Money (Ch. Wildflower Snapdragon, ROM, ex Ch. Marima's Keepsake).

CLANHEATH

Bryan and Gwynne McNamara bought Ch. Clancy of Clearwater (Hurlihy of Hopping Brook ex Lady Tara of Aspen Mill) from Constance Willis in 1974. From Marjorie Shoemaker they bought a bitch, Ch. Waterford Champagne Crumpet (Ch. Koop's Kilkenny of Woodridge, ROM, ex Ch Cloverlane's Connaught, CD) and started the Clanheath line.

A Clancy ex Crumpet breeding produced Ch. Clanheath's Misty Clover who in turn produced Ch. Jalin Clanheath in the Clover when bred to Ch. Wildflower Woodbalm, ROM, a Dandelion son. Clanheath in the Clover won the Roving Specialty in South Carolina in 1984 and was Best of Opposite Sex at the Metro Specialty in 1984, at the Roving Specialty in 1983 and at the Montgomery County show in 1982.

INTO THE FUTURE

It is only by looking back that we can develop some sense of where the breed is going. During the twenty-plus years since the O'Connors first imported Holmenocks Gramachree, Wheatens have changed significantly. The all-around Irish farm dog has now made its mark in the American show ring. At the same time, the Wheaten has increased in popularity as a family companion. These changes came about through the efforts of dedicated breeders and exhibitors who recognized the inherent qualities and charm that Wheaten owners treasure and managed to retain the best while improving and refining where they saw a need.

The dogs are more uniform in type. A longer, more rectangular head now predominates rather than the short, squarish head that was so common in the early years. The woolly standaway coat is not as prevalent as it once was. Structure and movement are greatly improved. Breeders are working hard to produce sound, true-to-type animals without losing the essence of the Wheaten.

110

Ch. Marima's Easy Money won Best in Show at Illinois Valley Kennel Club in May 1988 under judge Dawn Vick Hansen. Cindy Meyer was the handler.
Kathleen Kidd

BEST OF BREED
JANESVILLE, WIS.
MAY 7, 1977
OLSON PHOTO

Ch. Mellick Way Crackerjack, ROM, was a top producer whose offspring were top producers. He finished his title at six and a half months of age, a record for the breed.
Lloyd Olson

111

The geographic concentration of Wheatens has shifted to the west. Prior to recognition, the Wheaten Fancy was centered in the northeast. Today, finding a three-point entry in that area is not easy, but elsewhere in the country large entries are the norm.

The Wheaten Fancy has grown up, but this new maturity carries a bittersweet edge. Most Wheatens are still owner handled, but it is becoming increasingly clear that the services of a top professional handler are most valuable, particularly in Group competition.

The novices of the 1960s have grown in knowledge and stature. Newcomers seek their counsel and advice. The small group of long-time breeders who stayed the course have seen their dreams come true. Each time a Wheaten takes a Group first or a Best in Show, they can rightfully claim some of the credit.

Ch. Jalin Clanheath n the Clover won the SCWTCA Roving Specialty in 1984 and was Best of Opposite Sex at the Roving in 1983 and Montgomery in 1982 (pictured) under Richard Hensel.
John Ashbey

6

The Soft Coated Wheaten Terrier Club of America

BREED CLUBS are formed to preserve, protect and promote a particular breed of dog. Typically, a group of fanciers become acquainted and decide to organize. They contact known owners and solicit potential members. They write a constitution and by-laws. If there is no breed Standard, they write one. The members hold meetings and other kinds of events to achieve their goals.

When the American Kennel Club was new, it was simple for a breed club to become a member. One just applied. Now there is a set procedure that requires a number of steps through the various levels. If the club revolves around a miscellaneous breed, sanction is not possible until the breed is accepted into the Stud Book.

MISCELLANEOUS BREEDS

Acceptance into the Miscellaneous class is the first step toward AKC recognition for a breed that is not eligible for AKC registration.

A national club for a miscellaneous breed can only hold "fun" matches. These events have to be held in various parts of the country. The club also has to keep accurate records of dogs and breedings, including import pedigrees. Wide geographic distribution of dogs is a must.

When Lydia Vogel marched into AKC with her Wheaten pedigrees and photos, she had no idea what AKC requirements were. In fact, in 1947 the Miscellaneous class as it is known today did not exist. There was no list of eligible breeds. A showgiving club could decide which breeds could enter the regular classes and it was not required to offer classes for all recognized breeds. Any breed for which regular classification was not available had to be shown in Miscellaneous class. There was even a time when Miscellaneous class winners were eligible for further competition.

Today, breed fanciers must be well organized even to gain admission to the Miscellaneous class.

It was no wonder Lydia was disheartened by AKC's response of January 3, 1947, a portion of which is quoted here:

> Our rules for recognition of a new breed of pure bred dogs requires, among other things, applications for at least 25 dogs of a breed, the formation of a club for the purpose of forwarding the interests of the breed, a breed standard, etc. . . .

GETTING AKC'S ATTENTION

Lydia sent a letter stating that there was a club. She even submitted a set of bylaws. For numerous reasons, Lydia Vogel's efforts were unfruitful. Perhaps she was so overextended she was not free to devote herself solely to this goal. She bred and showed Kerry Blues, was a professional handler and had a grooming business.

FORMING A CLUB

Margaret O'Connor, however, had the energy and the desire to gain AKC recognition for the breed. Since a club was needed, she started one. On St. Patrick's Day in 1962 a group of Wheaten owners and three Wheatens met in the Brooklyn home of Professor Louis and Ida Mallory. The result was the formation of the Soft Coated Wheaten Terrier Club of America (SCWTCA). The first officers were:

Cover of the first issue of *Benchmarks* in its new format.

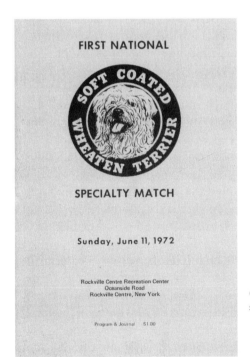

BENCHMARKS

PUBLISHED QUARTERLY BY THE SOFT COATED WHEATEN TERRIER CLUB OF AMERICA, INC
Volume 1, Number 1   FALL 1972

featuring:

- The Top Ten Wheatens

- Article by John T. Marvin
  noted judge and writer

- Grooming for the Show Ring

FIRST NATIONAL

SOFT COATED WHEATEN TERRIER

SPECIALTY MATCH

Sunday, June 11, 1972

Rockville Centre Recreation Center
Oceanside Road
Rockville Centre, New York

Program & Journal $1.00

Catalog from the first "fun match" sponsored by the SCWTCA.

President:	Margaret O'Connor
Vice President:	Ida Mallory
Secretary:	Eileen Jackson

THE NEWSLETTER

The club's initial act was to send out a newsletter. It was called *Wheaten Wires* and went to twenty-five Soft Coated Wheaten Terrier owners and supporters. By July, Margaret realized that the title was inappropriate for a "soft coated" dog so the name was changed to *Benchmarks* and is still published quarterly under that name.

When she chose the new name, Margaret explained that "a benchmark, according to Webster, is a point of reference from which measurements of any sort may be made. Since we hope to measure the growth and popularity of the Soft Coated Wheaten Terrier through this publication, we feel *Benchmarks* to be the appropriate name."

THE EARLY YEARS

The following year, Margaret's sister, Eileen Jackson, was elected as Secretary/Treasurer, an indication that there were club funds. There were so few members at this time that all efforts centered on locating more Wheaten owners. Maggie submitted articles to the major dog magazines, but since Wheatens were only in the Miscellaneous class, they did not make "hot copy." Still, Margaret persevered and had some success, notably her column for *Terrier Type*. Little emphasis was placed on formal meetings or bylaws.

The club concentrated on two activities: keeping the Stud Book and publishing *Benchmarks*. The club also published a small booklet about Wheatens and distributed it to interested people. The basic problem was that there simply were not enough dogs and owners to really have an active club. There was no mention of holding a Specialty match or show.

In 1963, when Margaret O'Connor wrote her first column in *Terrier Type*, she stated proudly, "There are now twenty-nine Wheatens known to be in the United States." Given the level of individual interest and the wide geographic dispersal of owners, it is understandable that the business of the club revolved around the O'Connors and a few friends who lived close to New York.

GROWTH AND STRIFE

But times were changing. A year after Margaret's death in 1968, as stated elsewhere, there were close to 250 Wheatens registered. This meant more club members since the breeders encouraged new owners to register their dogs and join the club.

A major factor leading to increased club activity was the extensive breeding done by the Arnolds and a few others. As people purchased dogs, they registered them with the Soft Coated Wheaten Terrier Club of America and joined the club. It was only a matter of time before someone would suggest holding a match.

Dog clubs lend themselves to contention. There always seem to be factions even in clubs of long standing and great stability. The Wheaten Fancy was and is no different. A small but influential group was dissatisfied with the way the SCWTCA was progressing toward AKC recognition. Rightly or wrongly, they aimed a certain amount of criticism at the O'Connors.

This "rebel" group recognized that there had to be Specialty matches. As they showed, they were exposed to exhibitors of other miscellaneous breeds such as the Shih Tzu, which had already gained AKC status, while the Wheaten remained in limbo. The Shih Tzu exhibitors informed Wheaten people how important matches were. The die was cast.

THE FIRST WHEATEN MATCH SHOW

On March 22, 1970, a Wheaten "fun match" was held in Rockville Centre, New York. There were thirty-five entries. Best in Match went to Leprecaun's Top Shoemaker (Gramachree's Minute Man, CDX, ex Marretthay's Irish Colleen) owned by Peter and Judy Siegel of Rockville Centre. John Cox was the judge.

The second fun match was held on June 6, 1971, again in Rockville Centre. It was hosted by the newly formed Soft Coated Wheaten Terrier Club of Metropolitan New York. Clark Thompson judged the entry of fifty-two Wheatens. Ch. Stephen Dedalus of Andover, CD, was Best in Match.

CHANGING OF THE GUARD

With the election of new officers for 1970, there was a significant change in the club's management. The O'Connors were no longer strongly represented on the board of directors. In the winter 1969 issue of *Benchmarks*, Mrs. Cecelia O'Connor and Eileen Jackson gave their final reports as president and secretary. Cecelia continued as editor of *Benchmarks* until 1973.

By opening the board to new participants from a wider spectrum, the club took another step toward fuller participation in the sport and moved closer to AKC recognition. In the process, the ongoing conflict about the coat and trimming surfaced again and again.

Though the club was founded in 1962, a constitution was not approved by the membership until 1968. A meeting held in November 1969 failed to bring in a sufficient number for a quorum and so no actions were taken. It turned out to be just an informal gathering with some heated discussion about the progress of the breed and the club.

THE O'CONNOR LEGACY

Without the O'Connor family the Wheaten Terrier's progress might have taken much longer. Their dedication produced the set of vital records that AKC required. Margaret, and later her mother, maintained communication with Wheaten owners and club members during the club's formative years. They encouraged others to show and offered trophies for Wheatens that won Obedience titles. In Eileen Jackson's last report as secretary, she quotes Casey Stengel talking about the 1969 New York Mets World Series victory. He said, "They came along fast but slow." What an appropriate statement!

The years 1970 to 1973 were years of rapid movement toward recognition by AKC. More people were showing their dogs. The Soft Coated Wheaten Terrier Club of America was giving Specialty matches. There was beginning to be some uniformity of presentation. However, there were differences of opinion as to what constituted "tidying" and just what was meant by a "neat outline." Wheatens were being shown in full coat and trimmed.

SURVIVING THE CHALLENGE

In 1971, a group calling itself the Breeder-Exhibitor Education Society (BEES) placed ads in the major dog magazines and mailed information to Wheaten owners and anyone else who contacted them. The SCWTCA then placed advertisements in those same magazines

Sherry Yanow (left) with Ch. Mt. Mellick's Devon Cream and Emily Holden (right) with Jenny Love of Addison Mews at the first AKC-sanctioned B Match at Macungie, Pennsylvania, November 1973.

Carol Carlson with Ch. Amaden's Joe Cotton Candy at the second AKC-sanctioned Plan A Match held at Rockville Centre, New York, in April 1975.

setting forth its own credentials as *the* national breed club. The BEES buzzed around for a while but its members eventually began to work through the Soft Coated Wheaten Terrier Club of America toward AKC acceptance.

At the time, the differences of opinion created a major issue among fanciers. Battle lines were drawn. It was trimmers versus non-trimmers. It is interesting to note that there is no longer any conflict about whether to trim or not. The question is how and how much. (More about trimming elsewhere.)

MOVING TOWARD AKC RECOGNITION

Another issue that came before the board was the idea of constitutional revision. It was never possible to have a quorum. The bylaws just were not adequate for a national breed club. Charles Arnold was largely responsible for suggesting changes. Most of his proposals were denied at first, but later the things he suggested went into effect. The club revised the constitution and bylaws and brought them more into line with AKC requirements in 1973 as a prerequisite for recognition.

Another somewhat minor controversy surrounded breed classification. There was a rather vocal group who wanted the breed to go into the Non-Sporting or Working group. As history shows, it was not successful.

Great credit must be given to the board of directors for maintaining a collective cool head during those crucial years of 1971 to 1972. The SCWTCA did not fall apart in spite of internal squabbling. In October 1972, President Tom O'Connor received notification from AKC that it was likely that the SCWTCA Stud Book might be accepted early in 1973. Reporting about an informal membership meeting in November 1972, Cecelia O'Connor expressed chagrin that little appreciation was shown for the efforts made by past members toward acceptance.

THE GOAL IS ACHIEVED

Now that recognition was at hand, instead of celebrating, the people continued to argue about trimming and control of the club. However, in spite of the conflicts, the goal was reached on March 13, 1973, when AKC approved the addition of the Soft Coated Wheaten

Terrier to the Terrier Group. Show eligibility was set for October 1, 1973.

The next goal for the club was to become eligible to hold AKC events. That approval came fairly quickly. The first Plan B sanctioned match was held on November 11, 1973, in Macungie, Pennsylvania and the second on June 15, 1974, in Livingston, New Jersey. On September 21, 1974, SCWTCA held its first required Plan A sanctioned match in Merion, Pennsylvania. The second A match was held on April 13, 1975, in Rockville Centre, New York. The club had completed all AKC match requirements and was eligible to apply for permission to hold licensed events, that is, shows at which points toward championships can be awarded.

THE FIRST WHEATEN SPECIALTY SHOW

SCWTCA held its first Specialty show in conjunction with the prestigious Montgomery County Kennel Club all-terrier show on October 5, 1975. Ch. Raclee's Express West O'Andover (Ch. Glenworth's Country Squire, ROM, ex Ch. Raclee's Serendipity) was Best of Breed. Best of Opposite Sex was Ryan's littermate, Ch. Raclee's Extra Special.

Holding a Specialty became the major event of the club's year, but there was other business to be accomplished. In 1974 the format of *Benchmarks* underwent a significant change. The publication had been mimeographed on 8½-by-11-inch paper and had no illustrations. In its new format, *Benchmarks* looked like a real digest-size magazine. It was typeset and had illustrations, photographs and advertising. Marjorie Shoemaker was appointed editor, a position which she held for ten years.

THE BREEDER REFERRAL SERVICE

That same year, the Soft Coated Wheaten Terrier Club of America started its breeder referral service. The service aimed to put people in contact with reliable member-breeders as a source for puppies. The board appointed a Standard revision committee headed by Gay Sherman.

In 1975, Jackie Gottlieb and Cindy Vogels undertook the publication of a newsletter, *Wavelengths,* designed to communicate timely information and official club actions to the membership.

The Breeder Referral Service became the Breeder Information Service. The "Shake Hands" brochure was introduced. The club aimed to give more information about Wheatens so that it would be easier for potential owners to decide if the Wheaten was really what they wanted. Work began on a code of ethics and an *Owner's Manual*.

SPREADING THE WORD

In 1976, SCWTCA held its first Roving Specialty in Colorado. That same year, the board appointed Jackie Gottlieb as the regular breed columnist for the *Purebred Dogs—American Kennel Gazette*.

The first few years saw SCWTCA grow in stature and activity. The club became involved in investigating and supporting research on genetic defects. The *Soft Coated Wheaten Terrier Owner's Manual* became a reality in 1979. A new Standard was approved in February 1982. SCWTCA started an eye registry and instituted the policy that breeding stock had to be OFA (Orthopedic Foundation for Animals) certified before owners could be included on the approved breeders' list.

In 1978 the board of directors approved a club logo, designed by Marjorie Shoemaker with Gay Sherman's help. The logo appears on club stationery and publications as well as trophies. It was cast as a pewter medallion that is given to any member whose dog becomes a champion.

DEFENDING THE GOOD NAME

The SCWTCA is dedicated to helping people locate sound, healthy Wheaten Terriers from reputable breeders who subscribe to the club's stringent code of ethics. As part of this program the club underwrites the cost of placing a club advertisement in the local newspaper when conditions warrant. This activity is coordinated with local clubs.

The American Kennel Club has high expectations for dog clubs holding events under its rules. Maintaining these standards is particularly crucial for parent specialty clubs. Becoming an AKC member club takes time and effort. A club has to have acceptable bylaws. It has to demonstrate a knowledge of AKC rules and policies. Its membership has to have a strong core of breeders and exhibitors. A specialty

The Soft Coated Wheaten Terrier Owner's Manual

Soft Coated Wheaten Terrier Club of America, Inc.

The SCWTCA *Owner's Manual* was first produced in 1979. The revised edition is available from the SCWTCA.

club is expected to educate the public and its members through articles in magazines, books and pamphlets. Perhaps the most significant task is that of keeper of the breed Standard.

AKC MEMBERSHIP

AKC's board of directors accepted the application of the SCWTCA to become a member club on September 13, 1983. Gay Sherman was appointed as the first delegate. The Soft Coated Wheaten Terrier Club of America continues to function as the official voice in matters regarding the Soft Coated Wheaten Terrier. It holds an annual Specialty and usually sponsors a Roving Specialty. There are two official publications, *Wavelengths* and *Benchmarks*. The address of the current secretary can be obtained by contacting the American Kennel Club, Inc., 51 Madison Avenue, New York, New York 10010.

7

The Wheaten
in Other Countries

THERE IS NO DOUBT that the great concentration of Soft Coated Wheaten Terrier activity today is in the United States. About a thousand Wheatens are registered each year by AKC. In 1989, there were 149 champions finished. There were twenty-three dogs that got Obedience titles. The ultimate award, Best in Show at an all-breed event, went to Wheatens three times. It is conceivable that had the breed not taken such a strong hold in this country, it could be on its way to extinction.

There are Wheatens in other countries, however. Dogs have been sent to England, Canada, Germany, Sweden, Finland and Australia from both Ireland and the United States. Sadly, Ireland, the birthplace of the breed, has almost no activity at present. Mrs. Holmes currently has only one Wheaten and the interest just is not there. The Irish lines are now dependent upon breeders in other countries.

ENGLAND

As we know, the Wheaten was recognized by the Irish Kennel Club in 1937. The most logical place for further development was of course England. English dogs of all breeds were shown in Ireland and the Irish showed in England. There was always contact among dog fanciers in both countries whatever external politics prevailed. Showing and breeding dogs cut across political, social and economic barriers. The sport of dogs is a great leveler.

A litter sister of Ch. Cheerful Charlie was sent to England in 1939 but no one knows what happened to her. In 1943, Mrs. Vardey of Sheffield imported two dogs and convinced the Kennel Club to recognize the Wheaten. Dr. Pierse supplied the history and Standard of the breed.

For years the Soft Coated Wheaten Terrier registrations were listed in the *Kennel Gazette*, the Kennel Club's official publication, under the heading of ''Any Other Variety.'' Wheatens were not granted championship status until 1973. Breeds must have at least 150 registrations and good representation at shows before they become eligible to win the much-sought-after Kennel Club Challenge Certificates. A standard of points was compiled and accepted by the Kennel Club in 1975. By the end of 1988, there were forty-four champions.

Challenge Certificates are allocated each year based upon registrations and exhibits at championship shows. Three CCs won under three different judges are required before a dog can become a champion. Only dogs that win CCs, Reserve CCs or first, second or third prizes in the open classes at championship shows will be entered in the Stud Book.

In 1955, Mrs. Corisande Read along with Miss Freda Barlow-Massicks and a handful of other fanciers founded the Soft Coated Wheaten Terrier Club of Great Britain. A year later, the club was registered with the Kennel Club. There are currently 450 members.

The first show held by the SCWTCGB was in October 1976. There were fifty-nine dogs in competition. In 1981, CCs were offered for the first time at a Soft Coated Wheaten Terrier Specialty show. As this event is held in the Midlands, another open show was held in the south in March 1981. A limited show (limited to members of the promoting club or to exhibitors within specific areas) was held for Wheatens in Scotland and Northern England in 1978.

Breeders, Past and Present

The dogs Mrs. Vardey imported were Cheerful Peter (Irish Ch. Charlie Tim ex Lambay Heroine) and Sandra (Eire's Leader ex Coolaura Lass). Dr. T. Murray imported Diana of Deohale (Silver Leader

Ch. Finchwood Irish Mist (Binheath Winston of Finchwood ex Binheath Mickle Miss) was the first English champion. *Infocus*

Ch. Clondaw Jill from up the Hill at Stevelyn (Finchwood Meadow Rue ex Clondaw Sweet Rose Price) was the top winning Wheaten bitch in England from 1985 to 1987.

Ch. Berkley Brockbuster (Ch. Lejerdell's Postage Paid at Falken ex M'Lady Mirthful Meggan) was the top-winning dog in 1988. *Russell Fine Art*

ex Wheatielocks) from Dr. Pierse. Peter and Sandra produced the first litter bred in England.

These were the war years and nothing of great import happened until 1946 when Fire Crest (Glenflesk Captain ex Cheerie Be) and Silver Spearhead of Holmenocks (Cheerful Charlie ex Silver Wheat) were imported by Lady Kitty Ritson and Mrs. D. C. Long.

Lady Kitty was well-known in dog circles. She was involved in other breeds and wrote several books. To have her take up this new breed was quite significant, as she had many contacts and was an acknowledged trendsetter. Fire Crest had his name changed to Glenguard Mournside Firecrest. Silver Spearhead of Holmenocks became Mournside McCoul. Firecrest won a Best in Show in 1946 at an Open show, that is, one which is open to all but where CCs are not awarded.

Many dogs with the Holmenocks prefix appear in the *Kennel Gazette* listings. Apparently dogs could be registered with the Kennel Club even though their owners did not live in England. Some of the dogs were actually transferred to other people, but a good number remained in the names of Maureen Holmes or her son.

Miss Freda Barlow-Massicks later owned Firecrest. He was bred to Glenguard Erris Lady (Mick Cosie ex Wheaten Lady) and created the main basis for the breed in England.

Miss Barlow-Massicks's kennel prefix was Glenguard. Dogs of her breeding became the foundation stock for Mr. Scargall's Lindumwold dogs. Tim of Lindumwold (Glenguard Mournside Firecrest ex Glenguard Moonshine) was transferred to Mrs. Corisande Read in 1950. In 1951, Mrs. Read obtained Lindumwold Christmas Eve (Glenguard Rambler ex Glenguard Moonshine). In March, 1952, a litter resulting from Tim and Eve was whelped. These were the first dogs to carry the Binheath name which dominated Wheaten breeding in England throughout the 1950s and 1960s.

Elizabeth Burgess used Finchwood as her kennel name. Mrs. Burgess is one of the major breeders in England. Her breeding began with Binheath Winston of Finchwood (Kelly of Binheath ex Kilndown Macushla), whom she obtained in 1965, and Binheath Becky (Kelly of Binheath ex Binheath Gili). She bred her first litter in 1966. She got Binheath Mickle Miss (Binheath Winston of Finchwood ex Kilndown Macushla) in 1967.

The Kilndown prefix belonged to Commander D. J. A. Heber-Percy. Kilndown Macushla (Seamus of Binheath ex Gay of Binheath) was the dam of Binheath Perro Benito, who was sent to the United

States in 1966 to Charles Arnold. Perro was a significant contributor to Wheatens in America.

Jo Hanton uses Plumhollow as a kennel prefix. She began her breeding in the early 1970s with Lockreen Clouded Yellow (Rufus ex Shuleen of Binheath). Her first litter was sired by Finchwood Rory McCool (Binheath Winston of Finchwood ex Binheath Mickle Miss).

Jo also owned Finchwood Florence of Rathmolyon (Binheath Winston of Finchwood ex Binheath Mickle Miss). Florence and Finchwood Wellington (Binheath Cedarwood ex Finchwood Rosalie) were the first Wheatens to earn Challenge Certificates in February 1975 when CCs were initially offered. The first championship was awarded to Finchwood Irish Mist (Winston ex Mickle Miss).

Imports from America

A number of Wheatens have been sent to England from the United States even though a six-month quarantine is an entry requirement for dogs sent to Great Britain from most other countries. Ch. Andover Lachlan Aspen of Piperslanding (Ch. Raclee Express West O'Andover ex Crackerjack Almond Joy), a dog bred by Jackie Gottlieb and Marilyn Van Maarth, was sent over in 1980. He became an English champion the following year.

Gleanngay's Ruffled Ribbon of Plumhollow (Ch. Gleanngay Holliday, ROM, ex Ch. Gleanngay Motown Magnolia), Ch. Windsong Prelude of Plumhollow (Ch. Wildflower Stardust ex Ch. Caleycrest's Amazin' Mazie) and Ch. Lejerdell's Postage Paid (Ch. Abby's Postage Dhu O'Waterford, ROM, ex Ch. Kate Dedalus of Forest Glen) are among other American Wheatens making their mark in England.

The Soft Coated Wheaten Terrier Club of Great Britain is expanding its activities and now holds health seminars. This is of great value in a small island country with a limited gene pool. The expense of a six-month quarantine is enough to daunt most breeders who might be considering importing dogs. Throughout the last thirty years, Ireland has been the source of large numbers of Wheatens because it does not have a six-month quarantine requirement.

Under these circumstances, breeders are limited in what they can do to eliminate inherited defects. Perhaps with the advent of frozen semen, breeders will someday have access to a reliable source of superior genetic material.

The English Standard

Approved by the Kennel Club 21 January 1975, Revised 1986. Reprinted by kind permission of the Kennel Club, 1 Clarges Street, Piccadilly, London W1Y 8AB.

General Appearance—Medium-sized, compact, upstanding terrier well covered with a soft, wheaten coloured, natural coat that falls in loose curls or waves. An active, short-coupled dog, strong and well built; well balanced in structure and movement, not exaggerated in any way. Standing four square with head and tail up, giving the appearance of a happy dog, full of character.

Characteristics—A natural terrier with strong sporting instincts, hardy and of strong constitution.

Temperament—Good tempered, spirited and game. Full of confidence and humour; a delightful, affectionate, intelligent companion.

Head and Skull—Flat, moderately long and profusely covered with coat which falls forward over the eyes. Skull of medium width but not coarse. Stop well defined, cheek bones not prominent. Distance from eyes to nose not longer, and preferably shorter, than the distance from the eyes to occiput. Jaws strong and punishing, muzzle square with no suggestion of snipiness. Topline of muzzle absolutely straight and parallel with skull. Nose black and large for size of dog. Head in general powerful, without being coarse.

Eyes—Clear, bright dark hazel. Medium size set under strong brow. Eye rims black.

Ears—V-shaped and folded at level of skull. Forward edge drops down slightly forward to lie closely along cheek, back edge standing slightly away from side of head. Leathers thin, small to medium in size, covered with coat and fringe.

Mouth—Lips tight and black. Teeth large. Jaws strong with a perfect, regular and complete scissor bite, i.e., upper teeth closely overlapping the lower teeth and set square to the jaws.

Neck—Moderately long, strong, muscular and slightly arched. Without throatiness. Gradually widening toward, and running cleanly into shoulders.

Forequarters—Shoulders long, well laid back, and sloping inwards from points to withers. Not loose, fine, but muscular. Viewed from any angle, the forelegs perfectly straight. Good bone and muscle. Pasterns strong and springy. Chest moderately wide. Dew claws on the front legs may be removed.

Body—Compact, with powerful short loins. Back strong and level. Ribs well sprung without roundness, providing deep chest with relatively short coupling. Length of back from point of withers to base of tail should measure about the same as, or slightly less than, from point of withers to ground.

Hindquarters—Thighs strong and muscular. Hindlegs well developed with powerful muscle and well bent stifles. Hocks well let down and turning neither in nor out. Dew claws on the hind legs should be removed.

Feet—Strong and compact, turned neither in nor out. Good depth of pad. Toenails black.

Tail—Customarily docked. Tail of fully grown dog about 4–5 inches long. Set on high, carried gaily but never over back. Not curled and not too thick.

Gait—Free, graceful and lively. Well co-ordinated with long, low strides. Reach in front and good drive behind, straight action fore and after. Head and tail carried high, the backline remaining level.

Coat—Soft and silky. Neither woolly nor wiry. Loosely waved or curly, but if curly, curls large, light and loose. The coat should not stand off but flow and fall naturally. Coat abundant all over body and especially profuse on head and legs. Length of leg coat sufficient to give good balance to the length of coat on head and body. There is no seasonal change in the length or texture of the mature coat. Over trimming or stylizing should be penalized. For show purposes the coat may be tidied to present a neat outline. Coat colour and texture do not stabilize until about 24 months and should be given some latitude in young dogs.

Colour—A good clear wheaten. A shade of ripening wheat. A white coat and a red coat equally objectionable. Dark shading on ears not untypical. Often a slight fluctuation in the intensity of colour in mature coat, but overall effect should be light wheaten. Dark overall colour and the even darker marking often present in the immature coat, should clear by about 18–24 months.

Weight and Size—Height: dogs approximately 18–19½ inches measured at the withers. Bitches slightly less. Weight: dogs approximately 35–45 lbs. Bitches somewhat less.

Faults—Any departure from the foregoing points should be considered a fault and the seriousness with which the fault should be regarded should be in exact proportion to its degree.

Note—Male animals should have two apparently normal testicles fully descended into the scrotum.

English Champions, 1975–1988

1975 Ch. Finchwood Irish Mist
Ch. Finchwood Paprika of Findarcy
Ch. Finchwood Florence of Rathmolyon

1976 Ch. Finchwood Fancy Free of Bacanti
Ch. Finchwood Wellington

1978 Ch. Bacanti Bierritz
Ch. Clonhill Caesar

1979 Ch. Plum Hollow Silver Cascade
Ch. Brownsbank Fin McCool of Glendowan

1980 Ch. Manyara Kericho of Keridown
Ch. Glendowan Garfield
Ch. Madame Cholet of Willowdown

1981 Ch. Piperslanding Oh Johnny
Eng. & Am. Ch. Andover Lachlan Aspen of
Piperslanding
Ch. Linksdale Alabama Hayrider
Ch. Keridown the Cobbler
Ch. Finchwood Faith of Findarcy
Ch. Glendowan Clarinda

1982 Ch. Plumhollow Sunshine Kid
Ch. Perlysiau Simmer Dim Miss
Ch. Linksdale Pussy Galore

1983 Ch. Hoehill Clonakilty Cluff
Ch. Bacanti Bill Sykes
Ch. Glendowan Clarissa of Keridown

1984 Ch. Caramel Cove Citrine
Ch. Bacanti Burlington Bertie

Ch. Clondaw Jill from Up the Hill at Stevelyn
Ch. Finchwood Tamarisk
Ch. Stapledene Deputy Dawg

1985 Ch. Bacanti Bayham Badger
Ch. Linksdale Sargent Bilko

1986 Ch. Plumhollow Seamus O'Flyn of Amonite
Ch. Stapledene Georgina

1987 Ch. Stevelyn King Creole
Ch. Cashmere Golden Flurry
Ch. Windsong Prelude of Plumhollow

1988 Ch. Clondaw Shea the Banshee
Ch. Berkley Brockbuster
Ch. Seamar Sparkling Star of Pindarique
Ch. Stevelyn Rock a Hula Baby of Erindanus
Ch. Finchwood Tawny Owl
Ch. Bacanti Blackboard Jungle
Ch. Clondaw Honey Badger

1989 Ch. Bacanti Bay City Roller
Ch. Plumhollow Calico Casey of Aletrips
Ch. Keridown Mile Failte (D)

1990 Ch. Stevelyn Tutti Frutti (B)
Ch. Stevelyn Us Male (D)

CANADA

After the United States and England, Canada probably has the most Wheaten activity and interest. The Canadian Kennel Club registers about 425 Wheatens, on average, each year. The breed was first registered there in 1979.

In 1975, Alan C. Fox, with Ruth and Gunther Appl, started the Soft Coated Wheaten Terrier Association of Canada. They lived in Regina in the province of Saskatchewan, which borders Montana and North Dakota. The Foxes owned Lustig's Benjamin Beachboy (Berdot's Casey O'Brien ex Butterglow's Blithe Spirit) and Carrie C's Peppermint Patty (Katie's Doctor Dhu Little ex Riverrun Carrie Colleen). The Appls owned Butterglow's Blithe Spirit (Ch. Duffy Muldoon ex Lady Gregory of Long Ridge) and Riverrun Canadian Hope (Lothlorien's Riverrun Strider ex Berdot's Sabrina Fair). They located about thirteen Wheatens that were in Canada at that time.

With the progress of the Wheaten in the United States it was only logical that the breed would cross the border to the north. While Canada is larger than the United States, its population is much smaller. This means that the interest in purebred dogs is spread among a smaller, more geographically widespread group. Fewer people means fewer dogs and fewer shows.

However, rarity seems to increase enthusiasm. The Soft Coated Wheaten Terrier was accepted for registration in Canada in 1978 and became eligible for showing in 1979. This was about three years after the first attempts to organize Canadian Wheaten owners. Compared to the thirty-year struggle in the United States, the Canadians can congratulate themselves on their accomplishment.

Wheatens were in Canada for years before the breed was recognized. A few that appear in the English records as being sent to Canada are: Binheath Nelson (Red Admiral ex Binheath Biddy) Binheath Rajah (Kelly of Binheath ex Binheat Biddy) in 1963 and Lockreen Sundance (Rufus ex Shuleen of Binheath) in 1971. Nelson went to Miss G. Lubitz, Rajah to Mrs. J. Gray and Sundance to a Mrs. Mactintosh. In 1975 Manyara's Dusty Bluebell (Finchwood Wellington ex Allanderry Wendy) and Noctanna's Teddy Boy (Wheatlodge Tobermory Boy ex Finchwood Breda Mickeen) added to the Soft Coated Wheaten Terrier population in Canada. None of these dogs was among the first Wheatens located by the early organizers.

Mrs. Maureen Holmes also sent dogs to Canada. Four were among the first Wheatens published in the fall 1976 club bulletin. They were: Holmenocks Haprilla (Holmenocks Hampstead ex Holmenocks Halmaska), Holmenocks Helitta (August Fancy ex Holmenocks Harlinka), Holmenocks Hapranna, littermate to Haprilla, and Holmenocks Heltra, littermate to Helitta.

Like the O'Connors in the United States, the Appls and the Foxes began by publishing a newsletter to establish a communications link with all known Wheaten owners. They mailed the first issue in June 1976. By November 1976, eleven families were on the membership list representing twenty-four of the thirty-five known Wheatens in Canada.

The first goal was to obtain Canadian Kennel Club recognition. The club needed a Standard, twenty-five registerable dogs and $100 (nonrefundable). The credo that was set down said, "Let's make the Soft Coated Wheaten Terrier a breed to be reckoned with, both as a family pet and as a show dog." As in the United States, the Wheaten was eligible to show in the Miscellaneous class at CKC events.

134

Am., Can. Ch. Holweit's Forget Me Not, bred by Sylvia and Bill Hamilton and co-owned by them with Naida Faircloth, is shown here taking top honors at the Rideau Terrier Specialty under judge Joseph Mecera. Trophy presenter is Fred Fraser.   *Paw Prints, Inc.*

In May 1978, a CKC official advised the club that Wheatens had been recognized by CKC. They would be eligible to enter shows in early 1979.

Am. Ch. Waterford Panama Gold (Ch. Koop's Kilkenny of Woodridge, ROM, ex Ch. Cloverlane's Connaught, CD) was the first Wheaten shown in a Canadian point show. He went BOB and Group first at the Ottawa Kennel Club on May 4, 1979. During this time club members held Wheaten "picnics" to promote interest in the breed and help owners learn to understand the needs of the Soft Coated Wheaten Terrier. They still hold this type of fun and educational event.

Alan Fox became the official registrar for the breed. He and the other SCWTAC members developed a code of ethics. He was the first editor of the newsletter. The bulletin was named *Wheaten Wags* in 1979. By May of that year, there were fifty owners representing seventy-five dogs. In less than a year, there were nine Wheaten Canadian champions.

In the 1980s, the association devised a constitution and bylaws. Members approved the code of ethics. The new goal was to be recognized by CKC as an official club. In late 1982, CKC gave approval.

The club grew and *Wheaten Wags* continued to be the link that joined the broadly dispersed membership. The next order of business was to encourage the formation of local Wheaten clubs. There is currently one local club that is officially recognized.

In April 1984, the SCWTAC held its first national Specialty in Montreal. James Reynolds of Ottawa, Ontario, judged the twenty-four entries. Brenmoors Hide and Sneak (Ch. Lontree Lasting Image of Cully ex Ch. Brenmoors Star Biscuit) was Best of Breed. Am., Can. Ch. Angelica's Hanz Solo (Ch. Jamboree Gleanngay Gaucho ex Am., Can. Ch. Legenderry Babe in Arms) was Best of Opposite Sex.

Wheatens in Canada have made great progress in a relatively short time with the breed placing frequently in the Terrier Group. In April 1981, Ch. Lontree's Borstal Boy went Best in Show at the Seaway Kennel Club.

There are close ties between breeders in the United States and Canada. Many familiar United States kennel names routinely appear in Canadian pedigrees, but Canadian lines are evolving. It will be interesting to follow how these lines develop as breeding moves further away from American stock. Conceivably, several generations from now, American breeders will use Canadian dogs to help their limited gene pool. In the meantime, the Canadian Wheaten Fancy is growing in numbers and sophistication and it is to be hoped that the trend will continue.

The Canadian Standard

Origin and Purpose—The Soft-Coated Wheaten Terrier originated in Ireland. It was an all-purpose working farm dog used for destroying vermin, hunting small animals, and guarding against intruders.

General Appearance—The Soft-Coated Wheaten Terrier is a medium-sized, hardy, well-balanced sporting terrier, covered with a soft, wavy, coat of clear, warm, wheaten colour. The breed requires moderation in all points and any exaggerated features are to be avoided.

The Soft-Coated Wheaten Terrier should present a square outline with the overall appearance of a steady, happy, well-coordinated animal who is alert to his environment and carries himself with a gentle dignity and self-confidence.

Temperament—Good-tempered, spirited, and game. Affectionate and loyal. Alert and intelligent. Defensive without aggression. He does not start a fight, but should always stand his ground; exhibits less aggressiveness than is sometimes encouraged in other terriers.

Size—Ideal height for males is 18½ in. (47 cm); for females 17½ in. (44 cm). Ideal weight for males is 35–40 lb. (16–18 kg); for females 30–35 lb. (14–16 kg). Deviations from the ideal should be penalized according to the amount of deviation from the ideal.

Coat and Colour—Abundant, single-coated, soft, silky textured, and gently waving. Neither woolly nor wiry, crispy nor cottony, curly nor straight.

Colour is any shade of wheaten. Upon close examination occasional red, white or black guard hairs may be found. However, the over-all colouring must clearly be wheaten with no evidence of any other colour except on ears and muzzle where blue-gray shading may be present. Puppies under one year may carry deeper colouring and some black tipping. The adolescent under two years may be quite light in colour, but must never be white nor carry grey, other than on ears and muzzle. In both puppies and adolescents, the mature, wavy coat is generally not yet seen.

Coat colour and texture do not stabilize until about two years of age and some latitude should be given in young dogs. However, the softer and darker puppy coat should not be preferred over the lighter and slightly harsher adult coat. For show purposes, the coat should be trimmed to present a neat terrier outline. Overstyling is to be discouraged and severely penalized.

Head—Well-balanced and moderately long with skull and foreface of equal length and in good proportion to the body. The *skull* is flat and not too wide. Cheeks are clean; moderate stop. The *muzzle* is square, powerful, and strong with no suggestion of snipiness. The *nose* is black and large for the size of the dog. *Lips* are tight and black. *Teeth* are strong and white, meeting in a scissor or level bite with scissors preferred. The *eyes* are dark hazel or brown, medium sized and well protected under a strong brow. Eye rims are black. Coat should fall forward over the eyes. The *ears* are small to medium in size, breaking level with the skull, and dropping slightly forward, close to the cheeks, pointing to the ground rather than the eye.

Neck—Medium in length and set well upon the shoulders, gently sloping into the back.

Forequarters—The Soft-Coated Wheaten Terrier should have a good reach in front. The shoulders should be well laid back with a clean, smooth appearance. The forelegs are straight when viewed from all angles and are well boned and muscled. Dew claws should be removed. Feet are round and compact with good depth of pad. Nails are dark, pads are black.

Body—The body is compact; the chest is deep but not round. The ribs are well sprung. The back is strong with relatively short coupling. Topline is level.

Hindquarters—The Soft-Coated Wheaten Terrier requires good drive from behind, so requires well-muscled rear assembly. The legs should be well developed with powerful muscles, well-bent stifles, turning neither in nor out. The hocks are well let down and parallel when viewed from behind. Dew claws on rear legs must be removed. The nails are dark.

Tail—The tail is docked so that two-thirds of its original length remains. It is high set, carried gaily but not over the back.

Gait—The gait is free, graceful and lively, having good reach in front and strong drive from behind, straight action fore and after.

Faults—The foregoing description is that of the ideal Soft-Coated Wheaten Terrier. Any deviation from the above-described dog must be

138

penalized to the extent of the deviation, keeping in mind the original purpose of the breed.

Disqualifications—*Overshot or undershot mouth; over-aggression; nose not solid black; yellow or light eye.*

Canadian Champions, 1979–1989

Amberwynd's Class Act
Amberwynd's Fancifree Dreamin
Amberwynd's Ramblin Rose
Amie O'Day
Andover Expressivo
Andover Butternut Jeffrey
Andover Harmony Ballade
Andover's Quiet Riot
Angelica's Hanz Solo
Angelica's Kiss Me Quick
Angelica's Plus One
Angelica's Whole Wheat Muffin
Armada Crackerjack Pure Gold
Artemus and Tigger Two of Riverrun
Artemus the Witch of Riverun
Astrancias Myshka Amberwynd
Ballykeel's Beau Geste
Ballykeel's Chatter Box
Ballykeel's I Will Follow
Ballykeel's Joie De Vivre
Ballykeel's Out of Pocket
Ballymena's Bruder Erie's Best
Ballymena's Shennanigans Gold
Ballynacally's Auntie Mame
Ballynacally's Eddy O'Eden
Ballynacally's Eden Princess
Ballynacally's Flamins Mame
Ballynacally's Honeyfitz
Ballynacally's Nomad
Ballynacally's Rebel Rouser
Bantry Bay Gleanngay Kairi
Bantry Bay Kalahari
Beauban's Tauni

Beauban's Thatcher
Beauban's Top Diggity
Beaugeste
Blarney's Elderberry
Bluestone's Charles Hawkins
Bluestone's Hooray Hooter
Bluestone's Man About Town
Bluestone's Sir Chancelot
Bradford Presents Sebastian
Brearah's Danny Boy
Brenden's Delightful Dene
Brenmoor's Bluenose Classic
Brenmoor's Hide and Sneak
Briarlyn Bold as Brass
Briarlyn Cedarton Look at Me
Briarlyn Gumdrop
Briarlyn Wild and Waggish
Broussepoil Alto
Broussepoil Bombadil
Broussepoil Bougainvilia
Broussepoil Canadian Whiskey
Broussepoil Capucin
Broussepoil Cashmere
Broussepoil Chablis
Broussepoil Chopin De Capucin
Broussepoil Demerarra Peluche
Broussepoil Don Quichotte
Broussepoil Duc D'Orange
Broussepoil Fanny De Peluche
Broussepoil Fantaisie Hanoux
Broussepoil Golden Bagatelle
Broussepoil Golden Tobby
Broussepoil Gout De Noiselle
Broussepoil Lady Mary Puplins
Broussepoil Maggie
Broussepoil Melba de Peluche
Broussepoil Merlin Enchanteur
Broussepoil Muscadet
Broussepoil Orange Becot
Broussepoil Pom D Api
Broussepoil Praline

Broussepoil Prince D'Orange
Broussepoil Soupcon Canelle
Broussepoil Tains Poilou
Broussepoil Tammy Mon Amour
Broussepoil Woodbalms Tammy
Bullseye's Irish Bugler
Bullseye's Irish Mist
Bullseye's Irish Moonbeam
Bullseye's Irish Solomon
Bullseye's Irish Whimsey
Bullseye's Whimsical Traveler
Butterglow's Allemande
Butterglow's Chauncey
Butterglow's Oonagh O'Kamerak
Butterglow's Tourdion
Cara's Dashing Dan
Cara's Irish Rose
Cara's Mary Go Round
Cara's O'Eric's My Joy
Cathandi's Irish Brandee
Chereh's Canada Fancy
Chereh's Irish Gentleman
Chereh's Shandy of Ash Manor
Chereh's Special Delivery
Chermar's Desert Sunshine
Chermar's Kinsale Caitlin
Cinder's Sneak Preview
Claypol's All American Boy
Clover's Paddy of Deva
Clover's Touch of Honey
Crackerjack Candy Cane
Crackerjack Ceilidh Duan
Crackerjack Enterprise
Desertsun's Abbey Chermar
Divine's Brian Boru of Cashel
Doubloon Incantation
Doubloon Innervision
Doubloon Lemon Drop
Doubloon's Hobgoblin
Doubloon's Prototype
Doubloon's Spun Gold

Dounam's Violin
Earlecroft Holweit Solid Maple
Earlecroft's Debut by Holweit
Elfinstone Amber O'Kuhullen
Elfinstone Angelfire
Elfinstone Callisto
Elfinstone Daughter of Time
Elfinstone Farley Moonrock
Elfinstone Irish Dandy
Elfinstone Morningside Sun
Elfinstone Wind Rover
Everglass's Buster O'Grady
Everglass's Just in Time
Everglass's Mischa Montgomery
Everglass's Skye O'Malley
Everglass's Wind Breaker
Fair Dinkum Airyn Celebrity
Finnigan's Andecker Andy
Finnigan's Felicity
Finnigan's Fireball
Finnigan's Flamboyant Fellow
Finnigan's Indelible Tramp
Finnigan's Splash O'Sophie
Finnigan's Sugar n Spice
Finnigan's Summer Serenade
Fleury Kuhullen Lil Dig'm
Flockati Perlin Pin-Pin
Flockati Pruneau
Gariann's Diamond Solitaire
Gariann's Golden Warlock
Gariann's Greenwood Minstrel
Ghillie's Bailey's Irish Cream
Ghillie's Dirty Harry
Ghillie's Irish Mist
Ghillie's Touch of Class
Ghillie's Waldo Pepper
Gleanngay A Different Dance
Gleanngay Moon Marigold
Gleanngay Motown Milestone
Gleanngay Motown Movin On
Glenkerry the Phantom

Goldenstar's Honey Muffin
Goldenstar's Hot Stuff
Goldenstar's Irish Blessing
Goldenstar's Irish Magic
Goldenstar's Sunshine Sassi
Greene Acre Gabrielle
Greene Acre Mandy O'Glenworth
Hallmark's Four Leaf Clover
Hallmark's Hey Crackerjack
Harwelden's Miss Dub Lyn
Hion Tangerine Dream
Hion's New Wave
Hion's Raggedy Ragtime Man
Holweit's Blaze of Glory
Holweit's Canadian Sunset
Holweit's Cinderella
Holweit's Creme De La Creme
Holweit's Dawn of Earlecroft
Holweit's Ddouble 'Llisious
Holweit's Ddouble Ddelight
Holweit's Ddouble Ddynamite
Holweit's Ddouble De Lluxe
Holweit's Ddouble Jjeopardy
Holweit's Earlecroft Initial
Holweit's Earlecroft Maple Key
Holweit's Fire Cracker
Holweit's Fire Works
Holweit's Firefly
Holweit's Flash Fire
Holweit's Honeymoon Sweet
Holweit's Maple Sugar
Holweit's Moonshine Whiskey
Holweit's Opening Knight
Holweit's Prince Charming
Holweit's Rapunzel
Holweit's Sleeping Beauty
Holweit's Sparkle Plenty
Holweit's Ssecond Gglance
Holweit's Ssecond Rreflection
Holweit's Sunbonnet
Holweit's Sunflower

Holweit's Ttwice Bblessed
Honeywood's Charisma
Honeywood's Oh My Goodness
Honeywood's Spinnaker
Irish Chessy
Jamboree Gleanngay Gaucho
Jancrest Ceasar's Salad
Janet's Misty Dawn
Jonelle's Bluestone Rhapsody
Jordan's Duff in the Ruff
Ka-lid's Adam
Kelly Irish Gibbons
Kenwood's the Rogue
Kilculen's Crackerjack Honor
Knocknahilla Pegeen
Kovaclaire Aongus Dundee
Kovaclaire Cinnimon Cinders
Kovaclaire Precocious Patty
Kovaclaire Ragabash Ceilidh
Kovaclaire Trooper MacGruder
Kuhullen's Bit O'Elfinstone
Kuhullen's O'Riley's Ceilidh
Lady Corneila of Fairfield
Lanajaki Megs Lisdoon
Legenderry Babe in Arms
Legenderry Baby Snooks
Legenderry Broadway Rhythm
Legenderry Smoke Signal
Legenderry Thunderbird
Lontree Major MacDuff
Lontree's Borstal Boy
Lontree's Boy O Boy
Lontree's Little Tomboy
Lontree's Lucky Amber Lace
Lontree's Tinsel Star
Lookinglass Barley Bree
Lookinglass Capricorn Cameo
Lookinglass Dana O'Darby
Lookinglass Rory O'Moore
Lookinglass Tobin O'Rourke
Love's Mystical Mist

Lustig's Bodor Smoky Topaz
Mapleglo's Premiere by Holweit
Marando's Prairie Sunshine
Marimas Chelsea Chit Chat
Marimas Classical Jazz
Mariners Tiernan
Mariners Unsinkably Molly
McDama Gleanngay Ms Got Rock
McGillicuddy Olympic Spirit
Miz Ceilidh of Pakenham
Moonbeam's Prairie Snowflake
Naturapath's Lovage
Neala Catalina of Perrydale
O'Casey's Kovaclaire Reel
Owendale's An Actor's Actor
Paddington's Bear Necessity
Paddington's Gil-Galad
Pakenham Auntie Mame Tribute
Pakenham's Blissful Bernadette
Penridge Wheaten
Pepperwood's Cap'N Crunch
Pepperwood's Caramilk
Pepperwood's Chips Ahoy
Pepperwood's Gaelic Mariner
Pepperwood's Ginger Snap
Pepperwood's Golden Grahams
Pepperwood's Rum'N Butter
Pepperwood's Shredded Wheat
Perrydale's Bossanova Bru
Perrydale's Cheeky Chacha
Perrydale's Foggy Forbes
Perrydale's Mister Snickers
Perrydale's Musketeer Mirage
Piranha Bulleye Captain Kid
Piranha Bulleye Irish Bliss
Piranha Bulleye Irish Bounty
Piranha Culzean Kc at Bat
Prairiecrest's Shining Star
Prairiecrest's Whirl Wind
Ragabash Catriona Clare Isle
Riverruns Cailin of Anlon

Riverruns Fagan O the Fields
Riverruns Prairie Anlon
Riverruns Tally Ho O'Mt. View
Sandman's Lone Ranger
Sandman's McGyvor
Sandman's Riverrun Caitlin
Shamrock Crackerjack Caper
Sunshine's Lad of Chermar
Tain's Broussepoil Funny Girl
Tain's C C Charlie C
Toulin's Here Comes Holly
Toulin's Kasey Kandu
Toulin's Peppermint Paddy
Tramore of Sunset Ridge
Waggish 'n Winsome O'Briarlyn
Waggish Briargreen HappyHart
Waggish Briarlyn HVNS Tbetsy
Waggish Flight to Phoenix
Waggish Most Happy Fellow
Waggish Over the Rainbow
Waggish Phoenix Fling
Waggish Rainbow Mist
Waggish Saucy Darlin O'Chereh
Waggish Starfire
Waggish Star Lite Star Brite
Waggish Tales of Merry Meg
Waggish Wil O'Briarlyn
Warwyck Tojo Peter Pumkin
Waterford Panama Gold
Waterford Westcoaster
Wavehill Mythic Magic Flute
Wavehill Stoic Star
Westland's Buttons and Bows
Westland's Feldhund Angie
Westland's Lindsay McGeeney
Westsong's Perrydale Presto
Wheathlee's Blarney Kaitlyn
Whimsical's Moonraker Express
Wildrose Krystal Image
Wildrose Tallyho's Pridenjoy
Wildrose Think I'll Keep Her

Windcrest Brady O'Beauban
Windcrest Casey O'Brookpark
Windcrest Shamrock's Charmer
Windcrest Tara O'Beauban
Windcrest's Killarney Chorus
Windquest Magicmaker of Zala
Windyflat's Whimsical Blonde
Wooden Regan O'Dale

WHEATENS ON THE EUROPEAN CONTINENT

There is a small but growing group of fanciers in Europe and Wheatens can be found in Germany, Sweden, Holland, Denmark and Finland. European shows are regulated by the Federation Cynologique Internationale, whose headquarters are in Belgium.

Finland

In Finland, the Wheaten Terrier Fancy has joined forces with Kerry Blue owners to form a club since there are not enough of either breed to support a single club. The Finnish breeders have produced a number of champions.

The first imports from Ireland were a bitch, Holmenocks Hepburn (Holmenocks Hackney ex Holmenocks Henrietta), from Maureen Holmes and a dog, Crecora Crepello (Holmenocks Grand Coup ex Croom Crespina), from Gerald Bourke. Both became International and Nordic Champions. These dogs were owned by Eve Coranda, who uses Geijes as her kennel name. Mrs. Coranda bred a number of breeds, including Kerries. Other Irish dogs that appear in Finnish pedigrees are Bennekerry Beachcomber (Holmenocks Hancock ex Hurley's Lass) and Holmenocks Himax and Himpara (Marretthay's Harvest Gold ex Holmenocks Himca).

English dogs also influenced the lines in Finland. Fuscus was out of Binheath Chloe by Farden Flanagan, a Swedish dog. Flanagan combines Holmenocks and Faraderry lines. International and Nordic Chs. Maddalo Jubilee Prince and Princess were sired by Eng. Ch. Clonhill Caesar out of Finchwood Allgold. They came to Finland in 1977.

Nearly all the dogs listed in the club's handbook trace back to this handful of dogs. The first imports came to Finland in the early 1960s

Swedish and Finnish Ch. Geijes Kilmore.

Newkilber Camelot.

Holmenocks Haffer
Holmenocks Hampsted
Holmenocks Harlinka
SUCH Holmenocks Hicklam
Nicola Gold Boy
Luck of the Sweep
Judes Pride
SF, MVA Geijes Kilmore
Tuusian Bonanza
Geijes Wheaten Higgins
SF, S, MVA Geijes Gingerbread
SF, SUCH Honeyrags Fallon
IRLCH Newkilber the Quiet Man
Newkilber Gilded Lily
Jetborne Felcot

Marretthay's Harvest Gold
Holmenocks Haffer
Holmenocks Himca
August Fancy
Kinnegolbrien
Miss Somers
Gussie's Pride
Newkilber Camelot
O'Callahan of Sunset Hill
Ch. Shaughnessy of Sunset Hill
Cobalt Bourtor Ballynilty
Roisin's Melina Halandri
Golden Barley
Jetborne Felcot
Holmenocks Halmaska

so the Finnish Wheaten history roughly parallels that of the United States. However, because of its size and population differences, the Wheaten Fancy in Finland is proportionally smaller.

Being relatively close to other European countries affords breeders in Finland an opportunity for frequent contact with fanciers all over Europe as well as in England and Ireland. This proximity will probably result in the development of a European "type" of Wheaten. Because Europe follows the Irish Standard, the dogs will most likely tend to look more like the earlier American Wheatens.

Germany

In her book *The Wheaten Years*, Maureen Holmes has little information on the Wheaten in Germany. However, in contacting Margaret Moller-Sieber, I was able to get some information about Wheatens there. She and her husband bred Kerry Blues before being introduced to Wheatens at Cruft's dog show in London in 1975.

Apparently, there were few dogs in Germany when Maureen wrote her book. According to Mrs. Moller-Sieber, in 1974 a dog from England, Wheatlodge Kevin Flynn (Holmenocks Horris ex Binheath Solera), was the first Soft Coated Wheaten Terrier registered. He was never shown or used at stud. In 1976, she imported Holloween Ail Mo Lurgan (Mulben Rover ex Jenny of Mulben) from Holland. This was her foundation bitch.

In 1978, the first German litter to have Mrs. Moller-Sieber's Wheaten Rebel prefix was whelped out of the Dutch bitch bred to an Irish import, Newkilber Camelot (August Fancy ex Ireland Ch. Roisin's Melina Halandri). There are twenty-two German champions and fifteen international champions with the Wheaten Rebel prefix.

One significant import from Ireland was the most titled Wheaten in the world, Newkilber the Quiet Man. He was the first Wheaten to win a BIS on the continent. Wheaten Rebel's Scarlet O'Hara, one of his daughters out of Int. D.VDH Ch. Wheaten Rebel's Honeysuckle Rose, is presently in the United States. She is co-owned by Mary Pickford and J. Langone.

Another prefix, Fantastic, used by Mrs. Beate Meinecke, is based on Waterford Blast Off and Waterford Jetsetter. A litter from those two dogs was born in 1982. Mrs. Meinecke also imported Ch. Lontree Waterford Wiggins (Ch. Abby's Postage Dhu O'Waterford, ROM, ex Ch. Waterford Lontree Lace, ROM) from Joy Laylon.

Other Irish dogs went to Germany from the Newkilber kennels

owned by two Americans, M. Prokosch and Jean Peterson. Onetime residents of Ireland, they now live in Minnesota.

Wheatens have also come to Germany from Austria and Holland. Dogs from Mo Lurgan, Red Oaks and de la Richesse in Holland appear in the registry. The Austrian dogs bear the prefix Airedy Castle.

In Germany, breeding rules are fairly strict. Bitches must be fifteen months old before being bred. As of February 1987, all dogs have to be X-rayed before they can be used for breeding and only dogs with good hips can be used. The rules are set by the Deutsche Klub für Terriers which was founded in 1894.

Holland

Wheatens were known in Holland as early as 1955, according to Maureen Holmes. Mrs. Beute-Faber imported some dogs from Mr. Mullens (Mulben) and began breeding. She was responsible for starting the breed in Holland. Her Mo Lurgan kennel name is widely known in Europe.

Some English dogs went to Holland in the 1970s. Among them were Neilglen Sheppy (Finchwood Zebedee ex Shivone Yarina), bred by Mrs. S. Bertram, who went to a Miss Stoppelenburg. She also obtained Finchwood Tansy, a bitch out of Finchwood Wellington ex Finchwood Irish Mist.

Currently, Jettie Albrecht is secretary of the Wheaten club in Holland. She uses the de la Richesse name that was mentioned in connection with Germany. She owned Ch. Gleanngay Gather Moonbeams, who died accidentally soon after she came to Jettie. Ch. Gleanngay Dhu'n Berry (Ch. Waterford's Bad Hobbit ex Ch. Gleanngay Holly Berry), a dog, is an important part of her breeding program.

Sweden

Hilde Nyborn has been most helpful in supplying the history of the breed in her country.

Wheatens first came to Sweden in the mid-1960s. There was no need for recognition by the Svenska Kennel Klub, as breeds recognized by FCI are automatically eligible for registration and championship competition. Nearly all dogs get registered. In the early years, about fifteen to thirty dogs were registered annually. There were some kidney problems, and the breed did not take hold at first.

In the 1980s, Swedish interest in the breed expanded dramati-

Newkilber the Quiet Man (Ir. Ch. Roisin's Morgan Hadlya ex Holmenocks Halmaska), owned by Margaret Moller-Sieber, is the most titled Wheaten in the world.

Int. Ch. Wheaten Rebel's Reach Out Ranee (Wheaten Rebel's Lord Nelson ex Wheaten Rebel's Aireen), also owned by Margaret Moller-Sieber, has Irish, German and Dutch ancestors.

cally. Ch. Lontree Lucky Star was the first U.S. import. Other dogs came from Ireland, England, Finland and Germany. The SKK currently registers about three hundred Wheatens a year, putting the breed in sixtieth place. Mrs. Nyborn points out that as a percentage of all dogs registered, the Soft Coated Wheaten Terrier is actually more popular in Sweden than in the United States. Most Wheatens are shown and entries at some shows run as high as thirty or forty dogs.

The Svenska Soft Coated Wheaten Terrier Klub was formed in 1977 and has about five hundred members. A newsletter predated the actual founding of the club. Britt-Marie Hok-Strom started this publication and she is considered the founder of the breed in Sweden.

Greta Niska imported the first dogs. They were: Binheath Sweet Blairney, who died soon after coming from England in 1965; Farden Flanagan, from Ireland in 1965; Binheath Chloe, from England in 1966; Geijes Wheaten Blondine, from Finland in 1967. All were bred and later came into the hands of Mrs. Hok-Strom.

Swedish shows feature a breeders' class in which a breeder shows four home-bred dogs. It is considered one of the most prestigious classes. The winners in each breed then compete in an all-breed BIS final. SKK maintains a ranking based upon placement and number of competitors. In 1990, the Fairylakes Kennel of Lena and Claes Carlsson from Göteborg were in second place at mid-year. The dogs they showed are sired by NUCH, SUCH, INTUCH Lontree Yankee Doodle Star out of NUCH, SUCH, INTUCH Fraser Tartan Pennsylvania Star, a daughter of Lontree Lucky Star.

Activities such as obedience, tracking, agility and search and rescue are much more popular in Sweden than in the United States. Mrs. Nyborn reports: "We have an annual 1,500 obedience entries as compared to the American 30,000—even though our total number of dogs is probably 5 percent of the total number of dogs in the U.S.!" Basic obedience is taught before even thinking about the breed ring.

Wheatens have had great success in obedience in Sweden. Mrs. Nyborn attributes their popularity in part to their ability to succeed in those activities mentioned above. Two Soft Coated Wheaten Terriers are obedience champions. The first one was LP, SLCH Swedewheat's Mulle who was followed by LP, SLCH Fraser Tartan Poetry in Motion. Another dog, Miranda, was the first Wheaten to be certified for search and rescue work. In tracking, Hardy is outstanding. SUCH Fraser Tartan Mr. Mods ranks near the top in forest search. In agility, Brosing's Jubilee Princess Ida, LP Lakkas Allamanda, LP SUCH Teiniledon Avustaja and Truly-Tillisch have achieved the best results.

Ch. Earnest Ernie de la Richesse, Ch. Orris Horace de la Richesse, and Ch. Gleanngay Dhu 'n Berry, three of Jettie Albrecht's Wheatens.

Lakkas Whizkid Broassis Benson, with an undocked tail.

Swedish and International Ch. Brosing's Jazz Express (American and Danish Ch. Andover Jazz Jubilee ex Swedish Ch. Major Wheat Up To Date), bred and owned by Ingrid Olsen of Vollsto, Sweden.

A group of Swedish Wheatens at play. The one on the left is LP, SUCH Teiniledon. Avustaja is practicing a water retrieve. Note undocked tails.

A breeders class in Sweden. NUCH, SUCH, INTUCH Lontree Yankee Doodle Star is shown with five of his get.

154

In the breed ring, a number of American dogs have attained Swedish titles. They are Brenmoor's Manifold, Carlinayers Buffalo Bill, Doubloon Hobgoblin, Lontree Lucky Star and Lontree Yankee Doodle Star. Other imports, not titled as of this writing, include Brenmoor's International Spy, Lontree Star Shine, Lontree Super Star, Rainbow's Razzle Dazzle, Gleanngay Rave On, and Wildflower Star Crossed Lover.

There is still some conflict about coat. People who have Irish lines won't breed to any dog that does not come from an Irish background. Because dogs are judged by authorities from different countries, the two coat types are both well represented in the ring. Tail-docking is illegal in Sweden, so the photographs in this section show dogs with and without docked tails.

Between judicious importing and use of artificial insemination, breeders in Sweden have made great strides. There is great concern over health problems, but the fancy in general seems to be dealing with them in a positive and constructive way. Entries at the national specialty are good and show a marked upward trend from year to year.

Standard of the Federation Cynologique Internationale

Country of origin: Ireland

Head—Long, in good proportion to the body, skull flat and clean between ears, not too wide. Defined stop, jaws strong and punishing. Foreface not longer than skull. Hair same colour as on body. Cheek bones not prominent. Head in general powerful without being coarse.

Teeth—Large, level or scissors, neither undershot nor overshot.

Nose—Black and well developed.

Eyes—Dark, dark hazel, not too large, not prominent, well placed.

Ears—Small to medium, carried in front, level with skull. Dark shading to ears allowed and not uncommon. "Rose" or "flying" ears are objectionable.

Neck—Moderately long and strong but not throaty.

Shoulders—Sloping, fine, well laid back, muscular.

Chest—Deep, ribs well sprung.

Body—Compact and not too long with powerful loins, thighs strong and muscular, hocks well let down.

Tail—Well set, not too thick, carried gaily. To be docked at ⅓ (one third) the total length, or cut after the 6th (sixth) joint assuming that this is in balance and proportion to the dog.

Forelegs—Perfectly straight viewed from any angle, good bone and muscle.

Hindlegs—Well developed with powerful muscle. Stifles bent. Hocks turned neither in nor out.

Feet—Small not spreading. Toenails preferable black but varying colours allowed.

Coat—Texture to be soft and silky to feel and not harsh. Young dogs to be excluded from this. Colour any shade from light wheaten to golden reddish hue. Trimming to be permitted.

Trimmed Dog—Coat to be close cut to the body at neck, chest and skull; to be especially long over eyes and under jaw. Whiskers to be encouraged. Profuse feathering on legs. Body to be trimmed to follow the outline of the dog. Tail to be trimmed close and neatly tapered.

Untrimmed dog—The coat at its longest not to exceed five inches. Abundant and soft, wavy and loosely curled. Abundance not to be interpreted as length. *Under no circumstances* should the coat be ''fluffed out'' like a Poodle or an Old English Sheepdog. Dogs shown in this condition to be heavily penalized as they give a wrong impression of Type and Breed.

Special attention is drawn to puppy coat development.

As pups are seldom born with correct coat of maturity, care must be exercised when assessing this point. They go through several changes of colour and texture before developing the adult coat. This usually occurs between 18 months and 2½ years.

Gait—Straight action fore and aft going and coming. Elbows tucked in. Side view: Free, light co-ordinated movement.

Appearance—A hardy, active, short coupled dog, well built, giving the idea of strength. Not too leggy nor too low to the ground.

Serious Faults—Undershot mouth. Excessive nervousness. Viciousness. Pale nose. White coat. Light yellow eyes. Any colour other than wheaten in body coat.

Character—Good tempered, spirited and game. Most affectionate and loyal to his owners. Most intelligent. A trusty faithful friend, defensive without aggression.

Pups are born true to type. They come reddish, greyish and sometimes clear wheaten. The masks are generally black. Sometimes there is a black streak down the centre back or black tips to the body coat. These dark markings clear away with maturity. No black is allowed in body coat at full maturity.

Height—Dogs: 18/19 inches at the shoulder. Bitches sometimes less.

Weight—Dogs: 35/40 lbs. Bitches somewhat less.

Note: The male animals should have two apparently normal testicles fully descended into the scrotum.

An example of a well-balanced Soft Coated Wheaten Terrier.

Three Irish cousins.

Note where the dog's shoulders are in relation to the handler's knee.

158

8

Soft Coated Wheaten Terrier Standard and Analysis

$\mathbf{A}$ BREED STANDARD is a word picture of the ideal dog. It is the responsibility of the parent club of each breed to set forth the criteria by which all dogs of that breed will be judged. The Standard provided here was approved by the Soft Coated Wheaten Terrier Club of America on February 12, 1983. It appears in the new AKC-approved format. The *italicized* amplification is based on the visual presentation of the Standard produced by AKC in conjunction with SCWTCA in the form of a slide show and videocassette. This audio-visual presentation is available from AKC and makes an excellent accompaniment to a study of the Standard.

GENERAL APPEARANCE

The Soft Coated Wheaten Terrier is a medium-sized, hardy, well balanced sporting terrier, square in outline. He is distinguished by his soft, silky, gently waving coat of warm wheaten color and his particularly steady disposition. The breed requires moderation both in structure and presentation, and any exaggerations are to be shunned. He should present the overall appearance of an alert and happy animal, graceful, strong and well coordinated.

The Soft Coated Wheaten Terrier's gently waving coat and easy nature impart a special image. While its Irish Terrier cousin is sleek, racy and hard coated and its Kerry Blue kin is more stylized and refined, the Wheaten is the casual country gentleman, more natural in trim and less aggressive in temperament. The Wheaten combines the verve and zeal of the terrier with the steadiness of the working dog, remaining true to its heritage as a member of Ireland's terrier clan.

All parts of the dog, from the rectangular head to the set-on of the tail, must present a picture of total balance. The term "well balanced" is important, for it is used throughout the Standard. It is the basis of proper Wheaten structure.

SIZE, PROPORTION, SUBSTANCE

A dog shall be 18 to 19 inches at the withers, the ideal being 18½. A bitch shall be 17 to 18 inches at the withers, the ideal being 17½. **Major Faults**: Dogs under 18 inches or over 19 inches; bitches under 17 inches or over 18 inches. Any deviation must be penalized according to the degree of its severity.

Square in outline. Hardy, well balanced. Dogs should weigh 35–40 pounds; bitches 30–35 pounds.

Moderation is a key element of the proper Wheaten. The Wheaten is a sturdy, workmanlike dog and must be well boned, but never coarse in appearance. In general, bitches are more refined and finer in bone than dogs.

The Wheaten is a medium-sized dog, and although there is no size disqualification, breeders should make every effort to produce animals that are within the desired range of height and weight. It is easier to breed up in size than to retain moderation. As a guideline, the withers of a properly sized adult male usually line up just below the knee of an average adult person.

HEAD

Well balanced and in proportion to the body. Rectangular in appearance; moderately long. Powerful with no suggestion of coarseness.

The wet-down head illustrates the head as two rectangles viewed from the side.

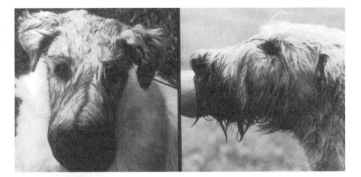

This dog has a proper-sized, well-set ear.

Note how the dark eye rim extends onto the skin surrounding the eye.

Stand-away ears are objectionable.

161

A rose ear.

Hound ears.

Button ears.

The large black nose protrudes beyond the fringe of hair on the face.

Scissors bite.

Level bite.

The head should be moderately long, neither cloddy nor over-refined and should be in proportion to the body. Picture it as one rectangle viewed from the front and two rectangles viewed from the side. The distance from the tip of the nose to the stop and from the stop to the back of the skull should be of equal length. There is a moderate stop. There should be sufficient length in each part so that the head has a rectangular rather than a square shape. The jaw must be powerful.

There should not be chiseling under the eyes or prominent cheekbones, as these detract from the rectangular shape of the head.

Eyes dark reddish brown or brown, medium in size, slightly almond shaped and set fairly wide apart. Eye rims black. **Major Fault:** Anything approaching a yellow eye. **Ears** small to medium in size, breaking level with the skull and dropping slightly forward, the inside edges of the ear lying next to the cheek and pointing to the ground rather than to the eye. A hound ear or a high-breaking ear is not typical and should be severely penalized.

The eyes should be brown, not black, and never yellow. The dark, reddish brown eye color predominates in the breed. The eyes should be slightly almond shaped, neither large and soulful nor small and hard-bitten. The eye rims must be black and in the mature dog, the black should extend onto the skin that surrounds the eye rims.

The ears must not stand away from the head. A rose ear is objectionable. Houndy ears are also undesirable as are high-set or button ears. The inside edge of the correct Wheaten ear should lie next to the cheek and point downward, not inward toward the eye.

Skull flat and clean between ears. Cheekbones not prominent. Defined stop. **Muzzle** powerful and strong, well filled below the eyes. No suggestions of snipiness. Skull and foreface of equal length. **Nose** black and large for size of dog. **Major Fault**: Any nose color other than solid black. **Lips** tight and black. **Teeth** large, clean and white; scissors or level bite. **Major Fault**: Undershot or overshot.

The large, black nose is one of the hallmarks of the breed. A brown or dudley (weakly pigmented, flesh colored) nose is a serious fault. The nose must protrude beyond the fringe of hair that covers the face.

In either a scissors bite or a level bite the teeth must meet with no open space between the upper and lower incisors. Crooked or misaligned teeth should be discouraged. Missing teeth should be penalized in accordance with the severity of the condition. Overshot or undershot mouths are major faults.

It must be noted that grooming plays an important role in the

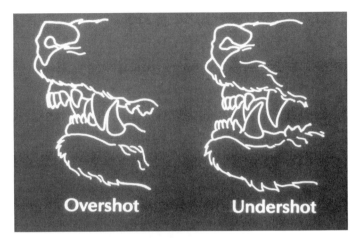

Overshot and undershot bites.

Overshot   **Undershot**

A well-groomed head. Here the eye is suggested, not exposed.

A poorly groomed head.

appearance of a Wheaten. Skillful trimming can enhance the appearance of a poor head just as poor trimming can spoil the appearance of a good head.

NECK, TOPLINE, BODY

Neck medium in length, clean and strong, not throaty. Carried proudly, it gradually widens, blending smoothly into the body.

Correct length of neck is important to achieving balance between head and body and providing a muscular base for efficient movement. The dog's neck should blend smoothly into the shoulder area. Here again, grooming can make a difference in the appearance of both set on and length of neck. While a longer neck may be aesthetically more pleasing, it is not as strong as the more moderate length of neck called for in the Standard.

Back strong and level. **Body** compact; relatively short coupled. **Chest** is deep. **Ribs** are well sprung but without roundness. **Tail** is docked and well set on, carried gaily but never over the back.

Keep in mind that the Wheaten should "appear" square in outline but is in fact slightly longer than tall. The rib cage is deep rather than round, and although well sprung is not barrel shaped. The ribs should reach to the elbow at the brisket and should have sufficient width for heart and lungs. The ribs taper to a moderate tuck up and the loin is relatively short. The topline is level from withers to set on of tail with no dip, roach or sway in the back. Ideally, a well set-on tail should stand at a right angle to the topline and should be in balance with the rest of the dog. The tail should not be so long as to be level with the back skull; rather it should be one half to two thirds the length of the neck. It should be neither too thick nor too spindly.

FOREQUARTERS

Shoulders well laid back, clean and smooth; well knit. **Forelegs** straight and well boned. All **dewclaws** should be removed. **Feet** are round and compact with good depth of pad. **Pads** black. **Nails** dark.

The shoulders should be close together at the withers. They should be well laid back to permit a long, free stride with plenty of reach in front. Upright shoulders or imbalance of the shoulder blade and the upper arm restrict front movement.

166

A good neck of moderate length, blending into the dog's body.

Note compact body, short coupling, deep chest and well-set-on tail.

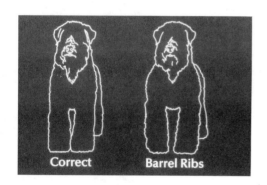

Correct   **Barrel Ribs**

Well-sprung ribs.

Too long in body.

Too tall.

Correct proportion of height and length.

Straight forelegs.

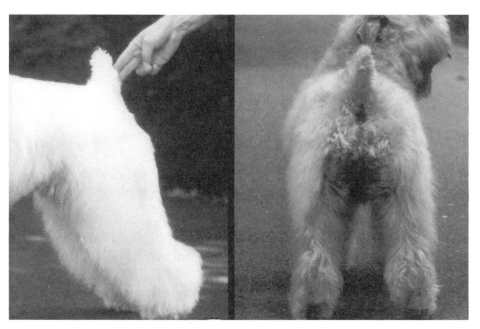

Well-bent stifles and well-let-down parallel hocks.

169

The forelegs form a straight line from elbow to foot. They should not turn in nor out, and in movement should form a single column of support.

Because of the coat, pasterns appear straight, but they should have a barely perceptible bend for shock absorption. They must be strong.

HINDQUARTERS

Hind legs well developed with well bent **stifles** turning neither in nor out; **hocks** well let down and parallel to each other. All **dewclaws** should be removed. The presence of dewclaws on the hind legs should be penalized. **Feet** are round and compact with good depth of pad. **Pads** black. **Nails** dark.

The hind legs are strong with rear angulation approximately the same as front angulation which creates a balanced appearance and smooth gait. The distance from hock joint to ground is short and the bone is straight. The feet are firm, strong and round, not hare footed or oval. A bad foot can sometimes be disguised by trimming so a judge should check the shape of the foot in addition to checking the depth and color of the pads. An oval shape would indicate less depth and strength. Black nails are preferred though tortoise is allowed. White nails are undesirable.

Cow hocks, sickle hocks and open hocks are all incorrect and inhibit proper movement. Good rear angulation as well as correct hocks are essential ingredients for good movement.

COAT

A distinguishing characteristic of the breed which sets the dog apart from all other terriers. An abundant single coat covering the entire body, legs and head; coat on the latter falls forward to shade the eyes. Texture soft and silky with a gentle wave. In both puppies and adolescents, the mature wavy coat is generally not yet evident. **Major Faults**: Woolly or harsh, crisp or cottony, curly or standaway coat; in the adult, a straight coat is also objectionable.

Understanding and defining proper Wheaten coat has caused more problems than any other aspect of the breed. It is vital to realize that the coat goes through various stages during the dog's life. The

A proper round foot with good depth of pads.

Cow hocks   Sickle hocks   Open hocks

Hock faults that interfere with proper movement.

Head coat falls so that it shades the eyes.

The dog in the background has a curly, woolly coat. The one in the foreground has a proper coat.

adult Wheaten has a single coat which is soft, silky and shiny. It should fall in loose waves or curls. There should be no tendency to a woolly or wiry texture. Puppies carry a soft, plush, dense coat with intense, rich color. As the Wheaten approaches adolescence his coat will often display less color and the texture will be a mixture of fine puppy hair and the more heavily textured adult coat.

After the age of two, the warm wheaten color and gentle wave should be evident. The adult coat is deeper colored than that of the adolescent, wavier and less dense. It lies closer to the body in loose waves. The difference is analogous to comparing the texture of a human child's hair to human adult hair.

Although proper coat is important, it must be remembered that color, quality, texture and condition of the coat are only individual factors in judging the entire dog.

PRESENTATION

For show purposes, the Wheaten is presented to show a terrier outline, but coat must be of sufficient length to flow when the dog is in motion. The coat must never be clipped or plucked. Sharp contrasts or stylizations must be avoided. Head coat should be blended to present a rectangular outline. Eyes should be indicated but never fully exposed. Ears should be relieved of fringe, but not taken down to the leather. Sufficient coat must be left on skull, cheeks, neck and tail to balance the proper length of body coat. **Dogs that are overly trimmed shall be severely penalized.**

The Wheaten should be presented in a more natural manner than most other terriers. Too much trimming must be penalized in the show ring. The head should be tidied to demonstrate the rectangular outline, thinning where needed to achieve a clean appearance. Eyes must not be exposed. The body coat is tipped and thinned to tidy the stray hairs and to smooth out areas of dense growth while following the outline of the dog. Blending is critical in order to avoid visible trim lines. The finished dog should look stylish and neat, but natural.

Author's comment: More and more Wheatens being shown are so stylized that they are beginning to look like blond Kerries with topknots like Dandie Dinmonts. The falls resemble visors. Exposed eyes really bother me. Until breeders, exhibitors and judges start to follow the Standard, the trimming will only become more extreme. We have a

A plush puppy coat.

A light adolescent coat.

A proper adult coat.

Some well-presented Wheatens
in the ring.

superb set of guidelines in the SCWTCA Grooming Chart. It is time to return to the kind of trimming that is unique to the Wheaten and is "stylish, neat and natural."

COLOR

Any shade of wheaten. Upon close examination, occasional red, white or black guard hairs may be found. However, the overall coloring must be clearly wheaten with no evidence of any other color except on ears and muzzle where blue-gray shading is sometimes present. **Major Fault:** Any color save wheaten.

Correct color is any shade of wheaten from pale blond to warm honey. There should be no other color anywhere except for blue shading on ears and muzzle which is fairly common but does not occur on all dogs. Either way is acceptable. Coat color changes throughout the life of the dog, but the Wheaten Terrier is always some shade of blond. The adult Wheaten should not be expected to carry the intense color of puppy coat nor must the coat ever appear gray, grizzle or white.

Puppies and Adolescents: Puppies under a year may carry deeper coloring and occasional black tipping. The adolescent, under two years, is often quite light in color, but must never be white or carry gray other than on ears and muzzle. However, by two years of age, the *proper* wheaten color should be obvious.

GAIT

Gait is free, graceful and lively with good reach in front and strong drive behind. Front and rear feet turn neither in nor out. Dogs who fail to keep their tails erect when moving should be severely penalized.

Correct assembly and balance of front and rear will enable the dog to move smoothly and efficiently. The Wheaten is a working terrier and thus requires reach in front and drive behind, permitting the dog to cover maximum ground with minimum effort.

Viewed in profile when moving, the Wheaten should look as though only the legs are moving. The body and topline should be carried along smoothly, neither bouncing nor rolling. The dog will tend to single track at faster speeds, but this should not be confused with moving too close behind or weaving or crossing in front.

Stylish, neat, natural.

Shaded and unshaded ears and muzzle.

175

This dog has reach and drive.

A group of Wheatens showing interest but not aggressiveness.

An efficient, balanced gait is one which will enable the dog to perform the tasks for which it was bred. Good front movement depends on a correct and balanced front assembly. The rear movement should be powerful with the legs forming a single column of support from hip to ground.

TEMPERAMENT

The Wheaten is a happy, steady dog and shows himself gaily with an air of self-confidence. He is alert and exhibits interest in his surroundings; exhibits less aggressiveness than is sometimes encouraged in other terriers. **Major Fault:** Timid or overly aggressive dogs.

The Wheaten is steady, merry and full of fun but should stand its ground when it is provoked. It should give evidence of a happy, stable temperament, never surly, timid or aggressive. Carried gaily erect, the Wheaten tail is an indicator of its happy nature.

SUMMARY

This brief discussion of the breed Standard is meant to provide some guidelines for breeders and judges. It is incumbent upon those who judge our breed to realize that the dogs to whom they award championship points will become the breeding stock of the future. Therefore, judges have a great influence on how the Soft Coated Wheaten Terrier develops and changes. However, the ultimate responsibility of maintaining breed type rests with the breeders. There will always be those who will breed to the day's top winner regardless of whether he complements a bitch or not. In the long run, it is the breeder who has a well-planned breeding program who will consistently produce sound, healthy and typey Wheatens.

Interpretation of a breed Standard is a subjective process. By studying the Standard, the AKC videotape, pictures and the dogs themselves, breeders and judges will be better able to continue the search for the ''ideal'' Soft Coated Wheaten Terrier as set forth in the official Standard.

These puppies still have their tails. The photo shows the shelf in the whelping box. The puppies are on indoor-outdoor carpeting.
Alan Goldie

This group of eager eaters are probably about a week old. Their tails have been docked.   *J. Alberts*

As the litter grows, the bitch no longer lies down for them to nurse.
Fred Kass

9

Breeding the Soft Coated Wheaten Terrier

WHEATENS are generally easy to breed. Bitches tend to whelp freely and puppies have sufficient weight and substance to survive without heroic efforts on the part of the breeder. Only rarely are bitches reluctant mothers. Caesarean section is uncommon.

THE DECISION TO BREED

This chapter is not meant to give detailed instructions on breeding and whelping. Other sources provide excellent information on this subject. It is intended to give enough information to enable a new Wheaten owner to decide if breeding and the attendant work is worth it. It might also remind experienced breeders about their obligations to the breed.

Breeding is not a project to be undertaken lightly. The problem of unwanted pets in the United States today is overwhelming. Unless you feel that you have a significant contribution to make to the breed and you can find good homes for your puppies, don't breed!

THE DEMAND FOR WHEATENS

The accompanying graph shows the progress that the Wheaten has made since it became eligible for AKC registration. Basically, growth has been slow and steady with a few years when new registrations actually declined. This is a healthy sign that the breed is not yet becoming a "fad." This may change, as in 1989 a prominent New York newspaper, *Women's Wear Daily*, touted the Wheaten as being the year's *in* dog. Serious breeders shudder at the thought.

When a person is deeply involved in a breed, it is only natural to proselytize about the breed's wonderful attributes to anyone who will listen, sometimes to great disadvantage. In the early days, owners were encouraged to breed their dogs just because they were Wheatens, and because AKC required sufficient numbers of dogs before it would consider acceptance.

In the 1950s and 1960s dogs were bred that perhaps should not have been. At that time, the breed had not attracted what is known as the seasoned dog fraternity. Most of the true terrier fanciers tended to look down on this shaggy upstart; some still do. Few Wheaten owners had experience showing or breeding. Knowledgeable mentors were few and far between, but by the 1970s that had changed.

THE KNOWLEDGEABLE BREEDER

Today's Wheaten Fancy is fortunate to have a strong core of dedicated, reputable breeders. Many have been active since the early days when everyone was still learning to play the dog game.

In a sense, they have grown up and become wiser and more sophisticated. They now use contracts when selling puppies and requiring spay/neuter agreements for pet-quality animals. They are much more careful of which dogs are bred. Their breeding programs are well planned. It is this small but tenacious group who will assure the future success and progress in the breed by passing their knowledge to newcomers and continuing to follow these self-imposed high standards.

THE RESPONSIBLE BREEDER

Responsible breeders recognize that the breed's future depends on the decisions breeders make regarding which dogs to breed. They

180

study pedigrees. They make an effort to see a dog's ancestors or at least to locate pictures. They know that they need time and sufficient, suitable space to raise a litter. They have the patience and the stamina to last through long hours of whelping and neonatal crises that may occur. They are members of SCWTCA and possibly a local club. Most of all, they are fully aware that only healthy Wheatens of superior confirmation and sound, stable temperament should be bred.

ECONOMICS OF BREEDING

Some people feel that they want to breed to recoup the cost of their dog. While Wheatens can be relatively expensive, if a buyer feels that he must get a payback by breeding, it might be better if he doesn't buy a Wheaten at all.

The expenses of raising a litter are large and constantly increasing. If your bitch has to be shipped to the stud dog of your choice, be aware that airline shipping has become more costly in recent years. If you want to use your dog at stud, be prepared to spend the money needed to show him to his championship title at the very least. Owners of bitches will not be lining up to use your dog unless he is a champion. They have too many other choices available to them.

Veterinary costs have soared. Both stud and bitch must be checked for congenital eye defects, X-rayed for hip dysplasia and tested for brucellosis. Tail docking, removal of dewclaws and inoculations add to the cost. If your litter should get some kind of virus, in spite of expert medical care, the puppies may all die. Can you and your family deal with that kind of loss? You will still have to pay the stud fee and veterinary bills even if there are no puppies to sell.

Advertising is another expense. It is unusual for all puppies to be spoken for by the time they are ready to sell. Even the best known breeders advertise. They do so regularly in the widely known specialized dog magazines. If you decide to follow that route, keep in mind that these publications normally have two-month lead times. Thus, you will be paying to advertise a litter than may or may not materialize.

WHY NOT TO BREED—MISINFORMATION

Many people think it is necessary for a dog or bitch to be bred in order to be fulfilled. This is just not so. A male, once used for breeding, may begin to lift his leg to mark his "territory," possibly including all your household furnishings he can reach. He may wander and often becomes more aggressive with other males. Breeding a bitch just so she knows what motherhood is like makes no sense at all. In the wild, animals breed for survival of the species. For domesticated pets, this need is no longer critical.

Breeding so that your children can witness the miracle of birth is not a good reason to breed. Books with graphic illustrations of whelping are easy to find. Videocassettes are now available that show the birth of all types of animals. Whelping can be a long process and few children can sit still for extended periods of time between births; your bitch does not need an audience. Besides, most children are just not interested.

WHY NOT TO BREED—PERSONAL DEMANDS

There is no end of work required in raising a litter. Be prepared to sleep in the whelping room for a few nights. The first seven to ten days in a puppy's life are critical. A newborn puppy has no way of regulating its body temperature and must be kept in a room that is maintained at a temperature of at least 85 degrees.

Puppies have to be weighed every day for the first ten days. Nails have to be trimmed weekly. Nine puppies equals thirty-six wiggly little feet. If mama does not or cannot fulfill her duties, you will have to take over and tube or bottle feed the litter and stimulate each one to make sure they are eliminating.

If your bitch does her job well, you are home free until the puppies are weaned at about four weeks. At that point, mother no longer cleans up after her brood. You are then in charge, and it is a constant job to keep the puppy pen clean.

This is a time when your family may begin to resent this interruption in their routine. Spouses and children will demand that the puppy area be sanitized before they will venture anywhere near it. Puppies wake up with the birds, so reconcile yourself to early mornings.

When it is time for prospective buyers to visit, you have to be there. Sometimes they will not show up at all. Again, your family will not be happy to give up their activities because you have to stay home.

When you are not caring for and cleaning up after the puppies, you have paperwork to complete—register the litter with AKC, prepare pedigrees, write up a complete set of detailed instructions, place advertisements and prepare sales contracts. (Sample sales contracts are available from SCWTCA.) This is a time-consuming job.

THE MECHANICS OF BREEDING

If you are not discouraged by the awesome prospect of becoming a responsible breeder, this next section covers some of the things that you will actually have to do. It will briefly discuss the care of the bitch and stud before and after mating, the mating, whelping and puppy care.

The Brood Bitch

Although a puppy gets half of its genetic makeup from each parent, the health of the bitch has a strong influence since fetal nourishment comes from her body and her maternal attitude affects that of the puppies. Ideally, the bitch is healthy and mature, sound in mind and body and has no major faults.

Health Checks

Wheatens come into season about twice a year. A bitch should not be bred until her second season, and it is better to wait until the third. If you have kept records of previous heats, you should know when to expect the next one. Bring her shots up to date and have a stool check done.

As close as possible to her season, have your veterinarian do a brucellosis test. Brucellosis is a highly infectious disease that is transmitted during breeding. It causes sterility.

While hip dysplasia is not a major problem in the breed, your dog should be X-rayed for it. Your vet is most likely familiar with the procedure for submitting the X-rays to the Orthopedic Foundation for Animals for evaluation. The OFA ratings are as follows: 1—Excellent, 2—Good, 3—Fair, 4—Mild dysplasia, 5—Medium dysplasia, 6—Severe dysplasia. Only dogs with a rating of 3 or higher should be bred. Dogs with 4, 5 or 6 grades should be neutered. Permanent OFA numbers are only granted to dogs over the age of two.

Another necessary health check is an eye examination to determine whether progressive retinal atrophy (PRA) is present. This test must be done by a canine ophthalmologist. The results are submitted to the Canine Eye Registry Foundation (CERF). If the eyes are free of the disease, a number is granted.

It is vital that breeders check their stock for these inherited disorders. By weeding out affected dogs before they are bred, conscientious breeders can help prevent the spread of these insidious conditions that have so seriously affected many other breeds.

Estrus

The first sign of estrus, or heat as it is commonly known, is a swelling of the vulva which can be observed during routine grooming. Check the bitch daily for the first signs of a bloody discharge. Count the days of her season from that first flow. Some bitches keep themselves so clean that you may have to simply wipe the vulva with a cotton ball each day to be sure. Some breeders test with diabetes paper to determine when she is ovulating. The size and softness of the vulva are indications of the progress of her season.

A season normally lasts about twenty-one days. This is often expressed seven days coming, seven days in, and seven days going. Confine the bitch for the entire time she is in season even after she is bred. An outdoor run is not safe. Males have been known to jump high fences to reach a female. I have even heard stories of dogs breeding through an opening in a crate. While she is in heat, walk her on a leash and keep her confined at other times, preferably in her crate. It could be a tragedy if she escaped through a door that was accidentally left open.

As soon as the bitch comes into season, have the vet test for vaginal infection. If one is present, there is still time to treat it before mating. All arrangements with the stud dog should have been made well in advance of her season. It is a good idea to have a backup stud dog in case your first choice is unavailable.

Shipping a Bitch

If you are shipping your bitch to the stud dog, time it so that she arrives at her rendezvous at the right time. Make the actual shipping arrangements at least forty-eight hours in advance, but consult the airline about their procedures even before your bitch comes into heat. Obtain an airline-approved crate and accustom her to it well before the shipping date. Attach an envelope to the crate that contains a copy of her brucellosis test results and instructions for feeding her.

If you plan to breed at the height of summer or in the depths of winter, you may have problems shipping. I am convinced that the airlines do not want to ship animals, since they set up such obstacles. Airlines will not carry animals unless the ground temperature at the shipping point and the destination fall within their guidelines. I once had to wait nearly two weeks to ship a dog to Montana in February. If you can find a suitable stud dog near enough for you to drive to, you can save time and money while protecting your bitch from additional stress.

The Stud Dog

The owner of the stud dog also bears a responsibility to the breed. One of the critical decisions a stud dog owner has to make is whether to breed to a particular bitch or not. It is not easy to turn down a stud fee, but breeding to a mediocre bitch doesn't enhance a dog's reputation. We are long past the time that every Wheaten was bred to swell numbers. Only those dogs that are of outstanding quality with something to give to the breed ought to reproduce.

The stud dog also needs proper nutrition and veterinary care as discussed in regard to the brood bitch. The stud should be mature and healthy with no serious faults. The same health checks apply to the dog as to the bitch.

It is slightly more important for a stud to be a champion than for a bitch. All others things being equal, owners of bitches will prefer to use a dog that has been evaluated by at least three judges and has been found to be worthy of a championship title.

The Mating

The usual practice is to bring the bitch to the stud dog. This means that the owner of a stud dog has to have facilities to keep a bitch confined for as long a it takes to get the desired number of matings. Typically, as soon as the bitch is receptive, mating is done every other day until at least two successful breedings occur. If air travel is involved, it is the stud dog owner's responsibility to pick the bitch up at the airport and make arrangements for her to be shipped back home.

The optimum time for mating is between the tenth and sixteen day but individual differences occur. Most bitches will readily accept a male during that time. Of course, there is an occasional bitch who will resist all advances by the male. Breeding my Lady Patricia of Windmill was always a struggle, but she conceived every time and was an excellent mother.

The first time a dog is used at stud it is better to use a bitch who has been bred before. This is no time to use a recalcitrant maiden who may injure the male. Do not just put two dogs in a room and hope for the best. Have a helper and put both dogs on leads. If the bitch seems snappy, muzzle her. Hold her firmly to allow the dog to mount her. When the penis enters the vagina, it expands and a muscle locks it in place. This is called the tie.

At this point the dog will normally dismount and turn so that the two dogs are tail to tail. He may need assistance. Do not let the bitch move or the male could be injured. After ejaculation takes place the erection subsides and the stud will pull out. Allow him to rest and if necessary, help him replace the sheath over the penis. Don't let the bitch urinate for several hours. Keep her crated.

Artificial Insemination

This is a procedure whereby semen is manually removed from the male and inserted into the female's vagina. It is used in cases where a natural mating is not possible. AKC will register litters resulting from AI breedings provided certain rules are followed: ". . . Both the sire and the dam are present during the artificial mating, and provided that both the extraction and insemination are done by the same licensed veterinarian." The proper form must be submitted with the litter application.

Artificial insemination can also be done with frozen semen. Again, policies have been set by AKC that cover the collection and preservation of semen. Only semen stored at approved collection centers can be used. Since there are not too many approved facilities, frozen semen is not used very often.

After breeding, keep your bitch close to home. She is still capable of being bred so make sure she is confined for at least another week. Try not to expose her to strange dogs. Never take a bred, or pregnant, bitch to a dog show.

Is She or Isn't She?

How can you tell if your bitch is pregnant? You have to assume that she is, provided there were at least two successful matings. She

186

may go off her feed for a few weeks but will become a voracious eater later in her pregnancy. She may vomit during the early weeks. My Kelly would just sleep. A sure sign of pregnancy was that she refused cheese.

This is a time when your knowledge of your bitch's normal behavior comes in handy. It is not to difficult to spot unusual patterns such as belching or increased need for sleep and affection. Experienced breeders can sometimes palpate and feel whelps during the fifth week but it is difficult, especially with a young bitch who carries high.

I do not feel that X-rays should be used to determine pregnancy. If she's pregnant, she is. If she isn't you can't do anything about it until her next season anyway.

Even your veterinarian cannot always tell. With my first litter, in her eighth week, I dutifully took Kelly to the vet just to see if everything was okay. My vet said there were no puppies. She had either resorbed them or was having a false pregnancy. I was devastated.

I completely ignored the fact that for several days I had been able to feel puppies moving when she was lying on her side. But if the vet said there were no puppies, he was the professional and he should know. Ten days later, she had eight lovely, healthy puppies and I changed veterinarians.

I learned three lessons from this harrowing experience. The first was that few vets have had experience with normal whelpings. They get all the problems. The second was to trust my own knowledge and instincts. The third was that a vet who understands the serious breeder is a treasure.

Care of the Pregnant Bitch

Offer a nutritious, well-balanced diet. (See section on diet.) Follow her usual pattern of activity. She knows best how much she wants to do. Avoid rough play during the last half of her pregnancy, but she will probably not want to be too active then anyway. If she is quite heavy with puppies, she will most likely need to relieve herself more often.

Whelping

Keep in mind that we are only hitting the highlights here. Consult one or more of the books on breeding that are listed elsewhere.

The dog's normal gestation period is about sixty-three days but may be as much as three or four days on either side. On about the fifty-seventh or fifty-eighth day from the first breeding, start taking your bitch's temperature in the morning and evening. When it begins to drop from its normal 101.5 you know that whelping time is getting close. This drop is to lessen the shock to the newborn puppies when they come into a world that hovers at 85 degrees. Her temperature can go as low as 90 degrees but this is rare. A bitch may shiver.

During the last week get your bitch used to the place where you want her to whelp. If you have the space, it is handy to have a fairly large whelping box that can serve until the puppies are ready to leave home. The one I used was four by four feet. The box should have a shelf or rail so puppies cannot be easily crushed by their mother against the sides of the box. Line the bottom with heavy plastic and several layers of newspaper. After the whelping, you can line the box with unbacked indoor-outdoor carpet. Place it in a quiet area or separate room where the temperature can be raised to at least 85 degrees. Have the following supplies at hand:

towels	scale
newspapers	nail polish
heating pad	notepaper and pen
thermometer	clock
alcohol	blunt-nose scissors
Vaseline	cotton balls
heater	

Wheatens are usually free whelpers, meaning they have uncomplicated, easy births. They take good care of their puppies. It is a rare bitch who is not a paragon of maternal virtue. Make sure your vet knows birth is imminent so he will be available if an emergency arises. As a rule, Wheatens have ample milk to feed their litters, but if the litter is large and some puppies are not thriving, consult your vet about using supplementary food. Early weaning may make it a bit easier on the bitch.

When birth is imminent, the bitch will pant heavily and contractions will be visible. If your bitch is straining without results for more than two hours, contact your vet. She will most likely scratch up the newspapers and bedding in the whelping box. She will lick herself.

In a normal whelping, the next thing that happens is that her water bag breaks. Soon a puppy in its sac appears. Be prepared to break the sac near the head so that the whelp can breathe. Let your bitch do as much as possible in attending to the puppy. She should

Soft Coated Wheaten Terriers are usually quite dark at birth and then they clear to the more familiar, typical color in a gradual process. The black mask is normal for month-old puppies such as this one.

Sue Goldberg

As Wheaten puppies grow, their coat and color undergo a number of changes. The black hairs recede and the coat takes on a change in texture from what it will be like in an adult. *Anita Roy*

Often in the course of maturing, a Soft Coated Wheaten Terrier's coat will become very pale in adolescence, later to regain depth of color in adulthood.

remove the sac and separate the umbilical cord. If she doesn't take the initiative, remove the sac and cut the cord about two inches from the puppy's body.

Most bitches will pitch right in, but if this is her first litter, she may not know what to do immediately. However, the instincts soon take over and the succeeding pups get her full attention. There is an afterbirth for each puppy. The bitch will consume the afterbirths if permitted. I usually allow her to eat two or three. The afterbirths seem to stimulate contractions and arouse maternal instincts. Every breeder has his or her own ideas about it.

Place the puppy at a nipple as soon as possible. This first milk (colostrum) provides immunity directly from the mother and is most important. Nursing stimulates uterine contractions. The bitch will lick the pup to dry it and stimulate it to breathe and eliminate. You can assist by gently rubbing the puppy with a rough towel. While she is whelping additional pups, place the dry ones in a box with a heating pad. A chilled puppy is a dead puppy. Keep the room at least 85 degrees for the first week.

Weigh each puppy and mark it with nail polish. Mark each one in a different spot and record it in your notebook. This will give you an individual chart on each pup. For example: male, left ear, twelve ounces, born first. The nail polish can be replaced if needed and it is safe to use. The chart will be a permanent record of the litter.

When she is finished whelping, she will rest comfortably, happily feeding her brood. Take her to the vet for a pituitrin or oxytocin shot within twenty-four to thirty-six hours. This injection stimulates uterine contractions and helps clean her out. Take someone with you in case she has another puppy in the car. Make the appointment at the beginning of office hours and be early enough to avoid contact with other animals. Feed her as much as she wants. She's worked hard and she deserves special treatment.

While she is nursing, check her breasts and nipples frequently. If there is any sign of soreness or caking, consult your vet.

Tail Docking and Removal of Dewclaws

Wheatens have long tails at birth. The tails are normally docked at three days of age. About one third to one half the length of the tail is removed. It is better to err on the long side as it can be redone. The current trend is for a longer tail to balance the somewhat longer necks that seem to be occurring with greater regularity. In the early days short tails were common.

Dewclaws are the vestigial remains of an extra toe. They are almost always present on the inside of the front legs and occasionally on the rear legs, although I have never seen them or heard of any one who has. If they are not removed, the nails grow long and the dog will chew at them. They serve no purpose in the Wheaten, and are best removed when the puppies' tails are docked.

Your vet should know how to handle tail docking. It is simple and relatively painless. Do it when the puppies are three or four days old.

Weaning

Most breeders start weaning their puppies at about four weeks. It is important to do this gradually so that the puppies' digestive tracts become used to a solid food diet. There is no hard and fast rule here. Each breeder has his or her own system and preference for handling this important part of a puppy's life.

I start my puppies on a fairly thin gruel made of one of the bitch's milk substitutes and baby rice cereal. It is served in flat pie plates and is slightly warmed. I start with the midday meal, trying to keep the mother dog away from the pups as much as possible during the day.

Once they are lapping well, I add some boiled chopped beef that has been whirled in the blender for a few seconds. I also increase the number of feedings to three times a day.

The next thing I add is ground puppy meal and gradually cut out the rice cereal. At least one meal contains cottage cheese. I give them scrambled eggs once or twice a week.

By the time they are six weeks old they are eating four solid food meals a day and mama only visits to play and eat up the leftovers.

Shots

Your puppies will get a series of inoculations to give them immunity to certain preventable diseases. Different veterinarians use different methods. Some breeders give their own shots. Personally, I prefer to rely on my vet.

You may be lucky enough have a vet who will come to your house. If you do have to visit the office, try to get an appointment at the beginning or end of office hours so that contact with sick animals is minimized or avoided. Keep the puppies in the car until the vet is ready to see them. Again, find a friend to help you. Keep a written record of the vaccines used and the date of inoculation.

Placing the Puppies

This is an area which has the potential for disaster. It is the responsible breeder's most crucial decision. By the time the puppies are seven or eight weeks old, the breeder is eager to have them in good homes. This is the ideal age to place a puppy because bonding with the new family is easier at that time.

It can be difficult to find suitable homes. People will see these adorable fluffy creatures and completely ignore the breeder's admonitions and advice about the management of the coat and the importance of training. It is a credit to the Wheaten personality that most dogs adapt reasonably well to a wide variety of familial situations.

Some breeders will not sell a puppy to someone without a fenced-in yard. Others do not want to place puppies in homes where everyone works, with some justification. Still others frown on Wheatens in city apartments. Some will not sell to a family without being assured the wife/mother truly wants a dog. All these concerns are justified.

In placing puppies, use a sales contract. Make sure as breeder that you are able, willing and, indeed, insistent on taking the dog back if the situation doesn't work out. There are cases where unscrupulous buyers obtain a bitch from a reputable breeder only to resell her to someone who operates a puppy mill. Such people will probably go elsewhere rather than sign a strict contract or just ignore it if it is signed. Fortunately, people like this are not common.

Having a contract with each buyer is more important than ever. You want to be sure that the puppy you bred is not going to be resold without your knowledge. This is one way that Wheaten puppies end up in undesirable hands. The AKC has recently established a nonbreeding registration. Please contact their offices for detailed instructions for using it. This is one of the best weapons we have in the fight against irresponsible breeding. If breeders screen potential owners carefully, good placement will be the norm. The demand for Wheatens is fairly high at present. Breeders should consider pricing their dogs so that a family with an average income can afford one. High prices encourage people to breed to get their investment back. People do call AKC to find out which breed is the most expensive so they can start a business breeding that breed!

Breeders must realize that not every dog is a potential champion. In Wheatens, even most of the champions are pets first and show dogs second. How fortunate is a breeder who takes a chance and places a quality puppy with a family, convinces them to show and encourages them to the point that they become active exhibitors. The Wheaten is still basically an owner-handled breed. The wise decisions of responsible breeders will determine where the Wheaten will stand in the dog world.

CONCLUSION

This chapter may seem to be a bit negative, but there is a purpose in this. If an owner is fully aware of the pitfalls and problems of breeding, he or she can make an intelligent decision about whether to breed or not.

This chapter is not meant to be a definitive discussion about breeding. There are numerous excellent books on the subject. Every breeder's library ought to have one or two. There is a bibliography in the appendix section of this book.

Ch. Marima's Classical Jazz winning an all-breed Best in Show. This is the ultimate goal for any dog that enters a show. *Booth*

Ch. Amaden's Whistlin Dixie, owned by James Brandt and Emily Holden, is shown winning Best of Opposite Sex at Montgomery County in 1985. Barbara Keenan is the judge. The handler is Carole Shefsky. *Dave Ashbey*

Group placings are highly sought after. Sue Goldberg and Ch. Brearah's Danny Boy are clearly happy about this win. The judge is John Honig. *John Ashbey*

194

10

Showing Your Wheaten

ONE OF THE MOST rewarding goals for the Wheaten owner to achieve is to show his Wheaten to its championship. If you have purchased a show-potential animal, take the time to learn about showing your own dog.

PLEASURES OF SHOWING

As you spend time grooming and training, you and your dog will develop a special relationship which grows over time. When you show, you will meet other Wheaten owners and expand your circle of friends while adding to your breed knowledge.

Showing is an enjoyable, gratifying activity, but it does require some preparation. In a show, the dog has to walk around a ring on a lead, tail up, in a pattern indicated by the judge. For the novice, this may seem to be a daunting proposition, but getting that championship certificate is well worth all the effort.

HOW AKC SHOWS WORK

To become an AKC champion, a dog has to earn fifteen points under three different judges. Two of the wins must be of three, four, or five points or "major" wins. Points are determined by the number of dogs defeated.

A dog is entered in one of five classes: Puppy, Novice, American Bred, Bred by Exhibitor and Open. Classes are offered for dogs and bitches. At Specialty shows, a twelve- to eighteen-month class may be offered and puppy classes may be divided by age.

The winners of each class compete against each other for Winners Dog and Winners Bitch. These dogs earn points toward their championships and can continue to compete with the champions entered for Best of Breed competition that day. Champions are often called "specials."

Within breed competition, Best of Breed (BOB) is the top award and the winning Wheaten is eligible to compete in the Terrier Group. The judge will also select a Best of Opposite Sex (BOS) to the Best of Breed dog and a Best of Winners (BOW). The Best of Winners dog or bitch gets the higher number of points available in either sex. If a class dog goes BOB or BOS, additional points can be won. No more than five points can be won at any show.

Point shows are always pre-entered. AKC can provide you with entry forms. After you have entered one or two shows, you will automatically receive premium lists (announcements) of upcoming shows from the superintendents. Subscribing to *Purebred Dogs—American Kennel Gazette* will bring you a calendar of events each month along with the magazine.

MATCH SHOWS

Before you start exhibiting in point shows, you should enter your dog in match shows. These are informal events where dogs, judges and exhibitors all gain experience. No points are awarded and puppies younger than six months may be entered. Entry fees are substantially lower than those charged for point shows. Since every AKC all-breed club must conduct one match for each year, there are plenty of opportunities for practice.

If your goal is to "finish" your dog (aquire a championship title), the more experience you and your dog have, the better your chances are of winning the points. If you prepare yourself and your dog, when you go into that ring you will both be comfortable and relaxed. Showmanship and condition matter a very great deal—especially in close competition.

Sweepstakes is an extra competition held at Specialty shows. Champions are not eligible and a percentage of the entry fees is given as prize money. Here, Ch. Amaden's Trapper John M.D. goes Best in Sweepstakes at the Parent Specialty under judge Marjorie Shoemaker. Emily Holden, co-owner, and handler James Brandt are also pictured.   *Dave Ashbey*

Best of Breed at a specialty show is to many as important as a Best in Show. Here Lynn Penniman handles Ch. Winquest Revelation at the SCWTCMNY show in 1979. The judge is Mrs. J. H. Daniell-Jenkins. Also pictured are Metro show chairman Bruce Goldsmith and Rose Vaccaro, owner.
Bernard Kernan

PROFESSIONAL HANDLERS

Wheatens are still basically an owner-handled breed. If you would rather have someone else show your dog, you can hire a professional handler. This is a person who is capable and experienced and earns his or her living by showing dogs owned by others in return for an established fee. Financial arrangements vary with the individual handler.

If you do take this route, be sure you have confidence in the person. Ask for references and check them out. There are organizations such as the Professional Handlers Association and the Dog Handlers' Guild whose members follow specific guidelines regarding their conduct. AKC can help you locate the current secretaries.

RING PRESENTATION

Another significant aspect of showing a Soft Coated Wheaten Terrier is ring presentation. Proper presentation goes well beyond the basic everyday grooming and trimming discussed in an earlier chapter. The following section on ring presentation was written by Marjorie Shoemaker, a longtime breeder and exhibitor. I am most grateful for her help. Follow her lead, groom your dog, go for that title and have fun!

DESIDERATA

The Soft Coated Wheaten Terrier is a challenge to trim for show presentation. The breed Standard uses the word "natural" in reference to appearance and grooming. Perhaps the term "naturalize" would be more appropriate. The coat should be left long enough to retain this more natural look, yet be tidy enough to maintain a terrier outline in motion or at those windy outdoor shows.

The Wheaten should never appear ragged, bunchy coated or heavy coated, the result of undertrimming or overtipping. When the dog is moving, this unevenness of coat is a distraction. Clumps of hair flapping in odd places or straggling where they should flow obstruct the appearance of good terrier outline and movement.

The look to be shunned is the clipped or tipped look where all the hair is shortened evenly to a terrier outline. The effect is that of a Bichon Frise or a Kerry Blue trim. This is incorrect and should be penalized in the ring although it is often seen. This "sculpted" puffy look is *not* natural. The effect should be one of easy lying of hair into gentle waves. The coat should waft (or flow) as the dog moves rather than bounce and pop.

The rule of thumb is to make the Wheaten appear to be naturally stylish; never should it appear unnaturally stylized. There should be *no* evidence of scissoring.

BASIC RULES

1. Have a picture of the ideal in your mind and use the hair to create this image.
2. Consider the dog as three-dimensional; the hair is your medium. Move around the dog and view areas from all angles as you work.
3. *Never* trim a dirty or matted dog.
4. Work slowly at first, taking time to check your work with the dog standing and moving on the floor.
5. Finalize your work by having someone stack and gait the dog; remove all the floppies, bunchies and whispies you see.

TOOLS

Thinning shears (hereafter referred to as shears to differentiate from straight-edged scissors)—Your most valuable tool, these shears create the more natural look by thinning and tipping. Single-edged shears are recommended over double serrated types.

Straight-edged scissors—This is used mainly to trim ear outlines, feet and, of course, low maintenance pet trims.

Comb—The Greyhound comb is a metal comb with narrow tines or teeth than can penetrate a thick Wheaten coat to the skin. Half the teeth are spaced closely—the other half are spaced slightly wider apart. This is a very important tool.

Pin brush—This is usually an oval-shaped brush with a rubber cushion in which pins are imbedded. It is used for blow-drying and brushing out the coat.

Slicker brush—This is rectangular and has a rubber cushion in which fine bent pins are imbedded. It is used for dematting and separating the coat.

Electric clipper (optional)—This can be used on the underside of the ear leather, between the pads of the feet and for cleaning off the stomach area. Its use requires some skill.

TERMINOLOGY

Tipping—The process of removing length of coat. Tipping also removes weight of coat and causes shortened areas to stand out or up, like a crew cut.

Thinning—The process of removing thickness of coat. This process will allow the weight of coat that is left to lie better.

Back-comb (or fluff-comb)—The process of combing an area of the coat backwards or out from the body to check the overall appearance and length of the coat in an area.

Blending—The process of graduating coat length and density from the closely trimmed areas around the underside of the neck and the rear of the dog to the longer coated areas along the sides and top. This technique is a vital part of creating the more natural look. It is a combination of tipping and thinning around the corners of the dog.

Popping—The effect of the coat standing out from the body. This occurs when a dog moves and is very evident if the dog is overtipped.

KEY POINTS

At the risk of repetition, the major factors in grooming a Wheaten properly are:

1. Have a strong mental image of your finished product. Your image should include covering or minimizing your dog's faults while enhancing the virtues. Use a photograph of a well-trimmed Wheaten if you have problems picturing the dog in your mind.

2. Use thinning shears to create a natural look and to avoid any appearance of scissoring.

3. Blend the short areas to the longer coat using the thinning-tipping combination.

4. *Never* cut across the hair; always use the shears following the direction in which the coat lies.

It cannot be emphasized enough that the proper way to groom a Wheaten is to "naturalize" the trimming by use of the thinning shears in the tipping-thinning combination. This is time consuming but in the end rewarding.

THE OVERALL OUTLINE

The first step is to stand at the side of the dog and "block out" the outline by working on the forequarters and then the aft. The area under the jaw at the start of the neck and down the front of the chest to the beginning of the legs should be trimmed fairly short. The rear profile from the tail down the rear leg and the slope to the hock should be trimmed rather closely as well. I use thinning shears for all of this unless the dog has not been groomed for a long time, in which case I would use straight blades, staying at least one half inch from the skin.

I return to the thinning shears to do the more precise trimming. After cleaning off both ends of the dog, step back and look at the effect. Decide where you want to locate the height of the topline to balance the length of the dog with the height. Take into account the length of the dog's neck and legs. Set the topline in with your shears.

Now the outline has been roughly set in. Proceed to work with your shears from the underside of the neck along the side of the neck and down to the shoulder. Tip these areas first, following the lie of the coat with your shears, not cutting across the coat. Thin the thick, bunchy areas by inserting the tips of the shears into the coat and next to the skin (again, in the direction the coat lies, not across the coat).

Some people might prefer using double-edged shears to thin because they can use a larger blade surface than just the tips of the single-edged shears. I have found that I alternate thinning and tipping techniques so often, that it would be a waste of time to change from one type of shears to another.

COMPLETE ONE SIDE AT A TIME

It has been my experience that it is better to work on one side of the dog before moving to the other. Keep working down and around the neck and shoulder area, blending the shortest hair along the underside of the neck gradually into the longest hair on the sides and top of the neck.

Wheaten in the rough.

Start by trimming fore
and aft of the dog to find
the outline.

202

Note that the hair growth around the neck tends to be rather heavy, no doubt to protect the jugular vein from attack. As a result, your work here will take some time, judiciously tipping and thinning this density, to avoid that heavily tipped or bunchy-coated look. Continue to work your shears along the sides, constantly looking back to what you have already trimmed, to check the smoothness from that angle.

Check the topline by back-combing. You will need to do somewhat more tipping around the withers, as the coat here tends to part and hang. You will need to do some thinning along the top of the loin area, as the coat here tends to be thicker and bunchy. Remember, tipping the entire topline will make the coat stand up and you will be left with areas that look as though your dog has a crewcut. This will not be compatible with the longer coat on the sides and will detract from the more natural look for which you strive.

Continue shortening and blending the coat along the croup and on the tail. Take care not to remove too much hair from the front of the base of the tail. Here again, you must blend the longer coat on the back to the base of the tail, and shorten the coat more toward the tip of it. Clean off the back of the tail, but keep in mind that you do not want the entire tail cleaned of coat, as it will then resemble a pencil sticking out of a haystack.

DON'T OVERTRIM

Having done your work along the neck, shoulders and the topline to croup and tail, check your work by grasping a small amount of hair between your thumb and finger on the other side of your dog. Pull the coat downward, then release the pressure (but not your grasp). Pull down and release again a few times, to create a rolling motion on the dog's side. This will "pop" the coat along the topline and side, allowing you to check the work. Beware of overtrimming! The more you shorten the hair, the more it will pop, so use the thinning technique to minimize popping. Tidy any stray strands if necessary.

The sides of the dog down to the tuck-up should carry a gradually longer coat. There will be less tipping and more thinning as you move downward. This will create a more natural look. This is the basic idea of blending.

Trim in the line of the brisket and tuck-up. A gentle curving line under the body is visually pleasing on a terrier. The coat should be the longest at the elbow, gradually sloping upward to the loin, creating the tuck-up and curving down to blend with the hair on the stifle. Too little or too much tuck-up will destroy the proper balance of the dog.

Again we want this to look natural, so do not cut across and make a "skirt" of hair all the same length. Point the shears down and at an angle toward the far side of the dog. Thin the coat when necessary with the shears under the dog, pointing up toward the dog's underside.

LEGS AND FEET

Legs and feet are the next objective. The front legs should appear as columns and a continuation of a straight line from the underjaw, down the neck and chest. The columnar effect is achieved by a slight flare of the coat below the knees and taper of coat back to the foot.

The coat needs a tight trim around the toes to give the "up on the toes" look desired in most terriers. To trim the feet, start by placing scissors flat on the table, under excess hair with the inside blade lying close to the foot. Open the blade, then tilt slightly so the outside blade rises from the table, and the inside blade is still on the table next to the foot. Proceed to cut around the circumference of the foot, removing any "snowshoe" effect. Tidy stray hairs, and tighten the circumference of the foot by using the blades at a greater angle from the table. Switch to thinning shears and round out the toe area.

Fluff-comb the leg, and with thinning shears pointing in the same direction that the coat would normally lie (either down or up), trim off excess in a columnar effect, retaining the slight flare around the base of the leg. Thinning may be required in the area of the elbow where hair can be more dense and also in the area on the inside of the leg from the knee down. Remember to work around the circumference of the leg for the columnar effect.

To check your work, pick up the leg by the toes and shake it. This will "pop" the coat. Tip and thin areas that do not lie correctly. Thin out bunchy areas. Don't try to tip them shorter. Work in a constantly moving arc around each leg to check all views of your column.

The rear legs are more complex in shape, due to the joints at the hock, stifle and pelvis (pinbones). It is your job to set in this angulation with the hair. The line indicating the stifle should be a gentle curve from the loin area to the front of the hock joint where it drops straight down to the toes. The hair covering the leg from the hock to the ground should form a cylinder when viewed from any angle. It should be

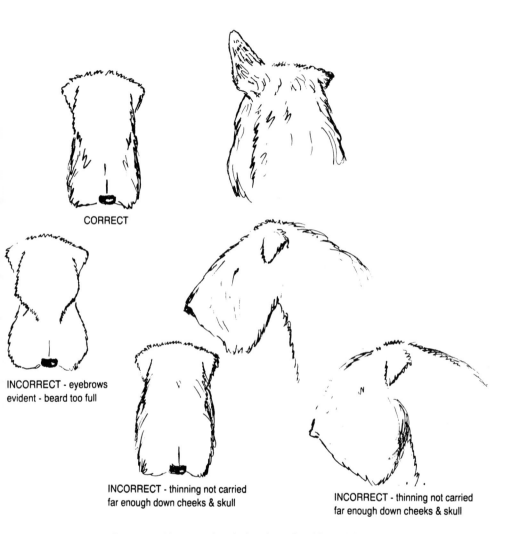

CORRECT

INCORRECT - eyebrows evident - beard too full

INCORRECT - thinning not carried far enough down cheeks & skull

INCORRECT - thinning not carried far enough down cheeks & skull

Correct and incorrect head trims from the side and the top.

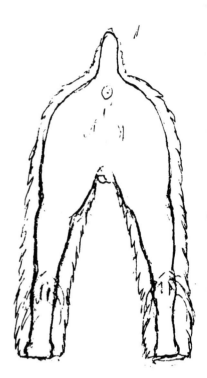

Correct trim from the front and the rear.

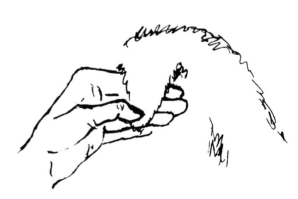

The correct way to hold the ear when trimming.

perpendicular to the ground. Be careful not to trim more than a perpendicular angle from hock to ground as this creates the impression the dog has sickle hocks.

On the aft, trim so that there is an indication of the pinbones. Be careful not to remove too much coat here or to leave too much of an indication, thereby creating a "shelf," an exaggeration to be avoided. Trim straight down from the pinbones to the second thigh (back of the stifle joint) and trim the second thigh, following the natural slope or angulation to the point of the hock.

From the rear of the dog, create a straight line on the inside of the rear legs by cleaning out the hair between the legs. More hair can be removed in the crotch area, as the hair forms a "skirt" here, but be careful not to remove so much coat as to expose the skin. The hair will be left longer along the inside of the second thigh to the hock to create a straight line. Thin the coat from the hock down to the ground.

On the outside of the rear legs, the hair forms "bloomers" over the hip and down to the second thigh, as it grows more densely here. This area requires a bit more tipping than thinning. However, some thinning is needed to avoid the scissored or sculpted look on the hips. The technique of fluff-combing is useful here, as it will simulate the pop of the coat when the dog moves. Make sure that you move around the rear of the dog to the side occasionally to check what needs blending from the rear to the side coat. You want to round off the corner of your dog between these two angles. Pick up the rear leg by the toes and shake it to see what areas need some tidying.

GROOMING THE HEAD

The last area to tackle is the head. Start by cleaning off the ears. Holding the edge of the ear between thumb and fingers and using your fingers as edge guides, trim the hair around the edge of the ear closely with straight-blade scissors. Be sure to always point the scissors toward the tip of the ear, to minimize the possibility of cutting it. Clean off the hair on the inside of the flap with straight blades or clippers.

With thinning shears, trim the hair on the outside leather. Hold the shears to point up toward the fold. It is helpful to lay the ear on the flat of your hand for support. The hair should be trimmed closely on the lower third of the ear. As you trim higher along the leather, allow the shears to head up and away from the leather, to gradually lengthen the hair. The hair at the fold should be left at least one third of an inch long.

Areas for close trimming on neck.

Properly trimmed Wheaten.

Stand at the side of the dog's head, fluff-comb the coat on the skull from the occiput to the brow (approximately one half inch above the eye). Lay the shears *parallel* to the plane of the dog's profile and trim in a straight line to the top of the skull coat. Now stand at the front of the dog and trim the top of the skull coat so it blends with the coat length on the fold of the ears. Carefully blend in the coat at the occiput area with the neck coat. Take care not to have too much coat on the topknot or not enough coat on the ears.

With thinning shears, thin out carefully down between the eyes in a V-shaped area, to remove the extra hair over and between the eyes that would obstruct the straight plane you wish to create from occiput to nose. The cheeks require thinning in a straight plane from the ears to the corner of the eyes. This area needs to be rather clean, but beware of overdoing or there will not be enough coat for blending.

To blend properly, allow the hair to get longer as you approach the corner of the eye. It may be necessary to thin or tip a bit down the lower side of the muzzle and into the beard in order to achieve the desired flat plane along the cheek. The corner where the skull and cheek planes meet should be removed at a 45-degree angle. Tip this area from the ear down to the brow and *carefully* over the eye. The eye should be indicated only by judicious thinning of the forelock. The eye should never be completely exposed or have a visor of hair over it.

As a finishing touch, thin out under the jaw area and toward the beard, again creating a straight line from the jaw to the point of the beard. You may need to thin, shorten and/or shape the beard by using the thinning-tipping technique. Now, check the dog while it is standing on the ground. Have someone stack the dog in show stance. Then have the dog moved. Trim away any hair that obscures or distorts leg movement, topline or any part of the dog.

COAT LENGTH

It is not possible to give the actual length of coat that would be left on any given area of any dog. The individual dog's coat and structure will be the determining factors. For example, change in coat texture and quality as the dog matures will require you to trim differently to achieve the desired results. A drop in the chest when the dog matures will necessitate more coat being removed in this area. The objective of the trimmer is to create a similar product from varied elements.

To reiterate, it is important that you have a mental image of what you wish to create. The goal in trimming a Wheaten properly is to *naturalize* your trimming by the combined thinning-tipping process. Naturally stylish—not unnaturally stylized!

11

Wheatens in Obedience

THERE IS nothing more pleasurable than living with a well-behaved dog. An obedient dog is under the owner's control at all times. The dog will sit, stay and come on command. These habits should be so ingrained that the dog responds to them instantly. A fast response in an emergency can be a lifesaver.

As the first domesticated animals, dogs have a special relationship with people. Basically, dogs want to do our bidding. They love to please their humans. Unfortunately, most people do not realize that in order for it to please us, we have to let the dog know what we expect of it. Communication between dog and owner is not easy. We train our dogs inadvertently to behave both well and badly.

Some breeds are more trainable than others. Wheatens tend to be more trainable than many other terriers but they are still not as tractable as Golden Retrievers or German Shepherds, for example. They are terriers and do need a firm hand.

One advantage of obedience training the Wheaten is that the dog and its owner develop a rapport that adds to the quality of the relationship. Nothing cements this unique partnership like learning together.

Dogs have a pack mentality. When the owner is the pack leader, the dog develops respect for him or her. When the dog is the pack leader, the owner lives in a state of fear and uncertainty about what the dog might do next.

A well-behaved Wheaten is a good advertisement for the breed. A trained dog is a welcome neighbor. It is to the owner's benefit to take the time and make the effort required to teach a companion dog basic obedience.

HOW TO FIND AN OBEDIENCE CLASS

On of the major duties of AKC-approved obedience clubs is to conduct training classes. AKC can help you locate clubs in your area.

The classes given by AKC clubs are based on the AKC requirements for the various obedience titles. The exercises gradually increase in difficulty and complexity as one advances from one title to the next.

AKC OBEDIENCE TITLES

In order to require an AKC obedience title, a dog must get three qualifying scores or "legs" under three different judges. A qualifying score is 170 or more points out of a possible 200 with more than 50 percent of the available points for each exercise.

The titles are: Companion Dog (CD), Companion Dog Excellent (CDX), Utility Dog (UD) and Obedience Trial Champion (OTCH). The two tracking titles are Tracking Dog (TD) and Tracking Dog Excellent (TDX). Except for OTCH, the abbreviations for obedience titles follow the dog's name. Only the highest title attained appears. Thus when a dog earns a CDX title, the CD is no longer used. The ultimate obedience title is OTCH (dog's name), TDX.

The first level in obedience is CD. The exercises and scores are:

1. Heel on leash and figure eight	40 points
2. Stand for examination	30 points
3. Heel free	40 points
4. Recall	30 points
5. Long sit	30 points
6. Long down	30 points
	200 points

These exercises constitute the Novice classes.

Gramachee's Minute Man, CDX, the first Soft Coated Wheaten Terrier to win an obedience title. *Mastercraft*

Holmenocks Gramachree, CD, won her title at the age of eight and a half years. She was the first Wheaten bitch to get her CD.

The next level is the CDX. These exercises are:

1. Heel free and figure eight   40 points
2. Drop on recall   30 points
3. Retrieve on flat   20 points
4. Retrieve over high jump   30 points
5. Broad jump   20 points
6. Long sit   30 points
7. Long down   30 points
                                 200 points

These exercises make up the Open classes. The long sit and down are done with the handlers out of sight.

The highest level is UD. The exercises are:

1. Signal exercise   40 points
2. Scent discrimination
   article #1   30 points
3. Scent discrimination
   article #2   30 points
4. Directed retrieve   30 points
5. Moving stand and
   examination   30 points
6. Directed jumping   40 points
                                    200 points

The title of OTCH can be obtained after a dog has a UD title. The dog continues to participate in Open and/or Utility classes. The title requires 100 points. The point schedule is determined by the class, Open or Utility, and the number of dogs competing. Points are earned for first and second place wins. For example, if a dog takes first in a Utility class with from ten to fourteen dogs competing, it gets six points. It is not an easy task to become an OTCH.

TRACKING

Tracking tests are held as separate events and a dog either passes or not. A track is laid and the dog is scored on how well it follows the trail and locates an article that was dropped by the track layer. The TDX track is longer and more difficult than the first level. As of late 1989, over a dozen Wheatens had obtained tracking titles.

Obedience competition is an activity that the whole family can enjoy. Joining an obedience club is a way to socialize with people and dogs. Getting "hooked" on training can lead to all kinds of rewards including titles, friendships and well-behaved, manageable dogs.

WHEATENS IN OBEDIENCE COMPETITION: EARLY YEARS

When dogs are in the Miscellaneous classes, they can, of course, be shown in conformation events. However, no points or titles can be won. Miscellaneous breeds can also participate in Obedience Trials and earn titles just as recognized breeds.

In the 1960s, the O'Connors became interested in obedience training. Margaret's sister, Eileen, trained Gramachree's Minute Man, CDX, to his CD title in 1964. "Rory" was the first Soft Coated Wheaten Terrier to gain an AKC obedience title. He got his CDX in 1966.

In 1965 at the age of eight and a half, Holmenocks Gramachree, CD, became the first obedience-titled Wheaten bitch. The O'Connors also put CD titles on Gramachree's Little Firecracker, CD, and Faraderry Fairy, CDX, in 1966. Gramachree's Paisteen Fionn finished her CD in 1968. Faraderry Fairy won her CDX in 1969.

Another Gramachree-bred dog, Gramachree's Roderick Dhu, CD (Gramachree's Minute Man, CDX, ex Faraderry Fairy, CDX), was trained by owner Suzanne Bobley to his CD title in 1968. "Max," as he was called, was the foundation of the Max-Well line. He played a role in the Mia Farrow–Dustin Hoffman film *John and Mary* in 1969. He also appeared on the well-known children's television show *Captain Kangaroo*.

The first Wheaten to become a UD was Rian's Captain Casey, UD (Gramachree's Deoch an Dorais ex Holmenocks Hascara) in 1980. In 1982 Templemore's Silk n' Ribbons, UD (Ch. Erinmore's Gleanngay Charley ex Ch. Gleanngay's Gwyneth) became the second Utility Wheaten.

OBEDIENCE WHEATENS COME OF AGE

In 1984, Moonstar Tory, UD, finished her Utility and TDX titles. She is the first Wheaten in the United States with both titles and has Canadian obedience titles as well.

Ch. Honeywood Dreamland Express, CDX, owned by Hermine Koplin, is a registered therapy dog. Her friends know her as Trumpet.

Stephanie Bee Koplin

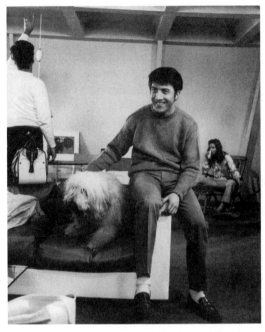

Gramachree's Roderick Dhu, CD, with Dustin Hoffman on the set of the 1969 20th Century–Fox film *John and Mary*. "Max" was one of the first Wheatens to be in show business.

Ch. Jan Ko's Erin O'Elfinstone, CDX, during the retrieve over the high jump exercise.

Janet Washko

Ch. Legenderry Baby Snooks has her CDX and TDX titles as well as championships in both Canada and the United States. She also has six champion get.

The above dogs are mentioned as examples of Wheatens that have had great success in obedience. We have yet to get the first Wheaten OTCH, but that too will happen. Since 1964, there have been 199 CD, thirty-five CDX, three UD, nine TD and two TDX Wheatens. Some of these are also therapy dogs. At least one is a qualified search and rescue dog. Another played the role of ''Sandy'' in a production of *Annie*.

Obedience training is beneficial for all dogs, large or small. All the dogs used in advertising and movies started with basic obedience training. There is no excuse for not teaching your dog to behave well. Earning a title is the icing on the cake.

Many of the dogs that gathered for the second Specialty of the SCWTCA (1976) shown here carried strong ties to the foundation stock that was so important to the rapid progress the breed has been able to make in the American show ring.

APPENDIX 1

Analysis of Foundation Stock Pedigrees

Going back to our foundation stock might seem to be irrelevant, but knowing where the breed started is important if for no other reason than it demonstrates how very small the gene pool is and how closely related the entire breed is. I am sincerely grateful to Sally Sotirovich for compiling this data and making it available to me.

Three Irish sires play an overwhelming role in the foundation of American Wheatens: Ir. Ch. Melauburn, Holmenocks Grand Coup and Holmenocks Hancock. The earliest of these three, Ir. Ch. Melauburn (Ir. Ch. Holmenocks Handley ex Holmenocks Hunch), whelped in 1952, sired **Gads Hill** and **Holmenocks Hallmark** as well as **Holmenocks Halyard,** a full brother to Holmenocks Hallmark. Another source of Ir. Ch. Melauburn in early breeding stock was his double granddaughter, **Faraderry Fairy, CDX.** A great granddaughter of Ir. Ch. Melauburn, **Pride of Marrethays,** played a significant role in many pedigrees. The last import to have a major impact on the breed, **Ch. Holmenocks Halpha,** was the daughter of Ir. Ch. Eden Prince, an Ir. Ch. Melauburn double grandson and a full brother to Faraderry Fairy, CDX.

In the mid-1960s, four significant imports sired by Holmenocks Grand Coup (Ir. Ch. Holmenocks Hartigan ex Ir. Ch. Holmenocks Herald) out of his half sister Croom Crespina (Ir. Ch. Holmenocks Hartigan ex Griselda) arrived that were destined to play a very large role in American Wheatens: **Croombour Crackerjill, Cobalt Bourcro Ballybay, Cobalt Bourtor Ballynilty** and **Bourcro Bantry Bay.** Another Grand Coup daughter, **Holmenocks Hallahuna** (out of **Holmenocks Hailsworth,** a full sister to Holmenocks Hancock), also appears in the pedigrees of American dogs. **Holmenocks Gramachree, CD,** found in so many pedigrees, was a half sister to Grand Coup and a full sister to Croom Crespina.

Holmenocks Hancock (Holmenocks Hackney ex Holmenocks Henrietta), a grandson of Grand Coup and a great grandson of Ir. Ch. Melauburn, had, along with his imported full sisters, **Holmenocks Hispaniola** and **Holmenocks Hailsworth,** a tremendous impact on the breed in this country through three of his offspring: **Blarney Blondie,** out of Honeycub Golden Dawn, and **Benker Belton** and **Bennekerry Beechnut** out of Hurley's Lass, a Grand Coup daughter. Mention must be made of Ir., Am. Ch. Benmul Belma, a full sister to Bennekerry Beechnut and Benker Belton, who, while her descendants in this country died out after several generations, will be remembered as the first Irish and American champion. Hancock is also felt in our pedigrees through his grandchildren **Holmenocks Haphazard** (a double grandson), **Holmenocks Harfore, Ch. Holmenocks Halpha** and **Limerick Jane.**

Three English Wheatens, whelped in the mid-1960s, are well represented in American bloodlines. They are **Binheath Perro Benito, Binheath Cushlamachree,** and **Cornbin Tanjareen.** All three are the offspring of breeding pairs based on two dogs: Tim of Lindumwold, whelped in 1948, and Lindumwold's Christmas Eve, born on Christmas Eve, 1950. Tim's pedigree is based on a single breeding pair, Glenguard Mournside Firecrest and Glenguard Erris Lady, while Eve's contains the same two with the addition of Betty of Deolali. Firecrest and Erris Lady were bred in Ireland before they were sent to England and are seen in the pedigrees of the great Irish sires mentioned above: Ir. Ch. Melauburn was a Firecrest grandson and an Irish breeding of Firecrest and Erris Lady produced Ir. Ch. Holmenocks Halo, the grandam of Ir. Ch. Holmenocks Hartigan, sire of Holmenocks Grand Coup, Croom Crespina and Holmenocks Gramachree, CD.

The imported dogs listed below are the foundation stock of the Soft Coated Wheaten Terrier in the United States. All of today's lines can trace back to the dogs listed here and a summary of the lines that emanate from each of them follows. In compiling this material, only the first four generations of descendants were considered. The dogs are arranged by relationship in chronological order based on whelping date.

IRISH IMPORTS

Gads Hill, 4/7/56, (Ir. Ch. Melauburn ex Ir. Ch. H. Herald)

Holmenocks Hallmark, 4/5/56 (Ir. Ch. Melauburn ex H. Hilite)

Holmenocks Halyard, 5/5/56 (Ir. Ch. Melauburn ex H. Hilite)

Holmenocks Gramachree, CD, 3/23/57 (Ir. Ch. H. Hartigan ex Griselda)

Pride of Marrethays, 11/9/62 (Ir. Ch. H. Hamish ex Golden Moss)

Bourcro Bantry Bay, 6/8/63 (H. Grand Coup ex Croom Crespina)

Cobalt Bourtor Ballybay, 6/8/63 (H. Grand Coup ex Croom Crespina)

Cobalt Bourcro Ballynilty, 6/8/63 (H. Grand Coup ex Crespina)

Croombour Crackerjill, 9/20/64 (H. Grand Coup ex Croom Crespina)

Holmenocks Hallahuna, 9/17/64 (H. Grand Coup ex H. Hailsworth)

Holmenocks Hailsworth, 8/14/63 (H. Hackney ex H. Henrietta)

Holmenocks Hispaniola, 5/6/65 (H. Hackney ex H. Henrietta)

Faraderry Fairy, CDX, 12/12/64 (Garfield Hiball ex H. Halcyon)

Bennekerry Beechnut, 12/11/66 (H. Hancock ex Hurley's Lass)

Benker Belton, 10/22/67 (H. Hancock ex Hurley's Lass)

Blarney Blondie, 4/6/66 (H. Hancock ex Honeycub Golden Dawn)

Holmenocks Helma, 1/3/70, (H. Hancock ex Ir. Ch. H. Hodella)

Limerick Jane, 8/10/69 (Garryowen Warrior ex Skagh Lass)

Holmenocks Haphazard, 10/14/71 (H. Horris ex H. Hamla)

Holmenocks Harfore, 8/4/72 (Freddie Klipper ex H. Hamla)

Ch. Holmenocks Halpha, 5/22/72 (Ir. Ch. Eden Prince ex H. Himca)

Holmenock Hascara, 1/16/73 (Ir. Ch. Eden Prince ex Ir. Ch. H. Hodella)

ENGLISH IMPORTS

Binheath Perro Benito, 10/24/64 (Kelly of Binheath ex Kilndown Macushla)

Cornbin Tanjareen, 10/20/64 (Kelly of Binheath ex Binheath Pooh-Ella)

Binheath Cushlamachree, 10/27/66 (Binheath Winston of Finchwood ex Kilndown Macushla)

GADS HILL

Dog, whelped April 7, 1956, by Ir. Ch. Melauburn out of Ir. Ch. Holmenocks Herald.

Gads Hill sired the July 4, 1962 litter out of Holmenocks Gramachree, CD, which produced his most influential offspring, Gramachree's Minute Man, CDX. Minute Man is represented in every line that emanates from his son, Leprecaun's Jackeen Arrah, sire of Ch. Stephen Dedalus of Andover, CD, ROM. One of Minute Man's daughters, Katie O'Cobalt, out of Holmenocks Hallmark, was the dam of Andover Antic of Sunset Hill ROM, Gallagher of Sunset Hill and Sunset Hill's Kilkenny Kate. Additional references to Minute Man are found under the other bitches he was bred to—Faraderry Fairy, CDX (G. Eivlin Aruin, G. Deoch an Dorais, G. Megread A Chara and G. Roderick Dhu, CD), Holmenocks Hispaniola (Leprecaun's Jackeen Arrah), and Croombour Crackerjill (Innisfree's Limerick Piper and Ch. Innisfree's Annie Sullivan, ROM). A litter sister to Minute Man, Gramachree's Little Firecracker, was bred to Bourcro Bantry Bay, producing Gramachree's Cruiskeen Lawn.

HOLMENOCKS HALLMARK

Bitch, whelped April 5, 1956, by Ir. Ch. Melauburn out of Holmenocks Hilite.

Hallmark's impact was based on two daughters, Katie O'Cobalt, out of Gad's Hill and Mocara of Sunset Hill out of Cobalt Bourcro Ballybay and a son, Callahan of Sunset Hills, also out of Cobalt Bourcro Ballybay. These offspring are dealt with in the sections on their sires.

HOLMENOCKS HALYARD

Dog, whelped May 5, 1956, by Ir. Ch. Melauburn out of Holmenocks Hilite.

A full brother to Holmenocks Hallmark, Halyard was bred in this country to Holmenocks Hailsworth. Three Grant's Hills dogs—Grant's Hill Lumberjack, Grant's Hill Yankee Trader and Grant's Hill Downeaster sired by Halyard out of Hailsworth, are found in the pedigrees of almost all American dogs. The descendants of these Grant's Hill dogs are found under Hailsworth.

HOLMENOCKS GRAMACHREE, CD

Bitch, whelped March 23, 1957, by Ir. Ch. Holmenocks Hartigan out of Griselda.

Since Gramachree was only bred once, to Gads Hill, references to her offspring are found under him. From this one litter came dogs that permeate Wheaten pedigrees.

PRIDE OF MARRETHAYS

Bitch, whelped November 9, 1962, by Ir. Ch. Holmenocks Hamish out of Golden Moss.

Pride produced the Egerluk dogs, Little Mermaid of the Egerluk, Towhead Charlie of the Egerluk, (by Cobalt Bourcro Ballybay) and Thistledown and Kiss Me Kate of the Egerluk (by Binheath Perro Benito). These dogs appear in the pedigrees of most of the major American lines.

Mermaid was the dam of Shamrock O'Perro of Brandy Keg, Brenock's Kelly's Luck Charm and Brenock's My True Kerry Love by Binheath Perro Benito. They are dealt with under their sire.

Thistledown, bred to Gramachree's Dermod O'Derry, produced Cloverlane's Clonmacnois, a foundation bitch for Lontree and her little sister, Ch. Cloverlane's Connaught, CD, a foundation bitch for Waterford.

Kate and Charlie produced Cloondora of the Egerluk, whose son Donegal Master Kerry carried the line to Erinmore.

BOURCRO BANTRY BAY

Dog, whelped June 8, 1963, by Holmenocks Grand Coup out of Croom Crespina.

Bred to Gramachree's Little Firecracker, Bantry Bay produced Gramachree's Cruiskeen Lawn, whose son, Stonecroft Evans, is found in Wildflower (Schnabel) and Sugar 'N' Spice lines.

COBALT BOURCRO BALLYBAY

Dog, whelped June 8, 1963, by Holmenocks Grand Coup out of Croom Crespina.

A littermate to Bourcro Bantry Bay, Ballybay was used extensively at stud. His direct offspring reach into nearly every Wheaten line through the offspring of four bitches—Katie O'Cobalt, Pride of Marrethays, Holmenocks Hallmark, and Cornbin Tanjareen that he was used on.

Bred to Katie O'Cobalt, he produced Andover Antic of Sunset Hill, the dam of Ch. Stephen Dedalus of Andover, CD, ROM, whose unquestioned importance is treated in the history section of the book. Gallagher of Sunset Hill, also out of Katie O'Cobalt, produced O'Callahan of Sunset Hills, Cavanaugh of Sunset Hill (Aspen Mill), Dungarvin of Sunset Hill, Roscommons Uncommon of Sunset Hill (dam of Jenny Love of Addison Mews, the foundation bitch for Amaden), Lothlorien's Riverrun Strider (Riverrun), Toby Mug of Sunset Hill who produced Gilchrist Gal O'Slievehoven (dam of Gilchrist's Dena of Waterford), Slievehoven Western Traveler (Glenkerry) and Slievehoven's Country Squire (Erinmore).

A daughter out of Katie O'Cobalt, Sunset Hills Kilkenny Kate, was the great grandam of Ch. Abby's Postage Dhu O'Waterford, ROM. Kate's son, Katie's Doctor Dhu Little, sired numerous Berdot dogs. Another Kate Daughter, Katie's Madame Dhu Barry, was the dam of Muffin's Miss Muffet, the Forest Glen foundation bitch.

Ballybay produced, out of Holmenocks Hallmark, a daughter, Mocara of Sunset Hill, who, when bred to Brenock's Kelly's Lucky Charm, produced a litter of three sons who were to leave their mark on the breed—Harrigan of Hopping Brook, Hogan of Hopping Brook and Hurlihy of Hopping Brook. Harrigan produced Ch. Glenworth's Country Squire (sire of Ch. Raclee's Express West O'Andover, CD, ROM, and double grandsire of Ch. Briarlyn Dandelion, ROM), Ch. Shandalee's Eric the Red and Ch. Glenworth's Andover Answer, ROM—all important sires and dams. Hogan appears extensively in Shandalee pedigrees and Hurlihy comes down through Clanheath pedigrees. Bred to Gallagher of Sunset Hills (see above), Mocara produced O'Callahan of Sunset Hill, sire of Ch. Innisfree's Annie Sullivan, ROM.

Used on Pride of Marrethays, Ballybay produced Little Mermaid of the Egerluk who was in turn bred to Binheath and Perro Benito. Mermaid's offspring are discussed under their sire.

Tanjybairn, a Ballybay son out of Cornbin Tanjareen, was used by the Leprecaun line which leads to Raclee, Mellickway, Windmill and Aspen Mill.

COBALT BOURTOR BALLYNILTY

Bitch, whelped June 6, 1963, by Holmenocks Grand Coup out of Croom Crespina.

A third offspring of Holmenocks Grand Coup and Croom Crespina to be imported to the United States, Ballynilty comes down to us through her produce by Gallagher of Sunset Hill (Dungarvin of Sunset Hill and Toby Mug of Sunset Hill). The descendants of her pups, Ch. Sweeney of Sunset Hill, Ch. Shaughnessy of Sunset Hill and Ch. Shiobhana of Sunset Hill, all by O'Callahan of Sunset Hill, have made significant contributions to the breed. Ballynilty bred to Shamrock O'Perro of Brandy Key produced Ch. Sunset Hills Galway Piper.

Amaden, Gilchrist, Chermar, Lontree, Waterford, Barryglen, Harwelden, Westridge, Everwill, Foxfire, Elfinstone, Kuhullen, Ballynally, Braemara and Slievehoven all trace back to Ballynilty through her son Dugarvin. Toby Mug of Sunset Hill influenced Gilchrist, Waterford, Riverrun, Slievehoven, Elfinstone, Glenkerry and Erinmore.

The following lines trace back to Ballynilty through her son Ch. Sweeney of Sunset Hill: Braemara, Glenkerry, Kuhullen, Elfinstone, Amberskye and Bomier. Another son, Ch. Shaughnessy of Sunset Hill is the grandsire of Int. Ch. Newkilber The Quiet Man. He also appears in Triconnel, Creme O'Wheaten, Terromari, Kuhullen, Erinmore and Knockahilla pedigrees. Ch. Shiobhana of Sunset Hill led to Erinmore, Rumstick, Lejerdell, Bundas and Glindale.

Ch. Sunset Hills Galway Piper appears in the pedigrees of Gilchrist, Riverrun, Glenkerry, Royale, Braemara and Jamboree.

CROOMBOUR CRACKERJILL

Bitch, whelped September 20, 1964, by Holmenocks Grand Coup out of Croom Crespina.

The fourth of the Holmenocks Grand Coup x Croom Crespina offspring to have a very significant place in Wheaten history is Croombour Crackerjill. Bred to Gramachree's Minute Man, CDX, she produced Innisfree's Limerick Piper who was the foundation dam for the Max-Well line. Bred to O'Callahan of Sunset Hill (Gallagher of Sunset Hill ex Mocara of Sunset Hill) she produced Ch. Innisfree's Annie Sullivan, ROM, whose contributions are discussed in the main text.

HOLMENOCKS HISPANIOLA

Bitch, whelped May 6, 1965, by Holmenocks Hackney out of Holmenocks Henrietta.

A full sister to the great Irish sire Holmenocks Hancock, Hispaniola, bred to Gramachree's Minute Man, CD, produced Leprecaun's Jackeen Arrah whose progeny figure in most of today's lines. Her presence permeates American Wheaten pedigrees and is thoroughly discussed in the main text.

HOLMENOCKS HAILSWORTH

Bitch, whelped August 14, 1963, by Holmenocks Hackney out of Holmenocks Henrietta.

Another full sister to Holmenocks Hancock, Hailsworth bred to Holmenocks Halyard produced Grant's Hill Lumberjack, the grandsire of O'Hagan's Cindy of Ashworth, dam of Ch. Koop's Kilkenny of Woodridge, ROM. Another son, also by Halyard, Grant's Hill Yankee Trader, sired Lady Gregory of Long Ridge, Butterglow's foundation bitch. Long Ridge Aileen Aroon is a Yankee Trader daughter who produced the Glocca Morra line now being carried on through Harriean. A Hailsworth daughter, by Grant's Hill Downeaster (Holmenocks Halyard ex Holmenocks Hailsworth, Grant's Hill Ocean Melody, was a Berdot foundation bitch whose great grandson was Ch. Abby's Postage Dhu O'Waterford, ROM.

HOLMENOCKS HALLAHUNA

Bitch, whelped September 17, 1964, by Holmenocks Grand Coup out of Holmenocks Hailsworth.

Hallahuna, a Hailsworth daughter by H. Grand Coup, bred in Ireland, was bred to Gramachree's Cruiskeen Lawn, producing Stonecroft Evans who was discussed under Bourcro Bantry Bay.

FARADERRY FAIRY, CDX

Bitch, whelped December 12, 1964, by Garfield Hiball out of Holmenocks Halcyon.

A double Melauburn granddaughter, Fairy produced four off-spring by Gramachree's Minute Man, CDX, who gave rise to lines which still continue today. Her son, Gramachree's Dermod O'Derry was the sire of the Cloverlane bitches, who are discussed under their grandam Pride of Marrethays.

A daughter, Gramachree's Evilin Aurin, was bred to Benker Belton and produced two daughters, Ch. Tammara of Balitara, CD, the foundation bitch for Legenderry, and Byrdie of Balitara, found in Chermar.

Gramachree's Roderick Dhu, CD, was the great grandsire of Ch. Abby's Postage Dhu O'Waterford, ROM. Many Berdot dogs trace back to his son, Katie's Doctor Dhu Little. Dhu Little's full sister, Katie's Madame Dhu Barry produced Muffin's Miss Muffet, the foundation of Forest Glen. He was also used by Max-Well.

Gilchrist's Deoch An Dorais was the grandsire of Berdot's Bridgette, dam of Ch. Abby's Postage Dhu O'Waterford, ROM. Deoch was the main sire used in the Berdot lines.

BINHEATH PERRO BENITO

Dog, whelped October 24, 1964, by Kelly of Binheath out of Kilndown Macushla.

Perro was one of the three English imports. He was widely used at stud by the early breeders. A relatively small number of his offspring have had a significant impact on the breed.

Used on Pride of Marrethays, Perro produced the Egerluk bitches, Kiss Me Kate of the Egerluk, and Thistledown of the Egerluk who are discussed under their dam.

Bred to Little Mermaid of the Egerluk, a Cobalt Bourcro Bally-bay and Pride of Marrethays daughter, Perro produced two dogs—Shamrock O'Perro of Brandy Keg and Brenock's Kelly's Lucky Charm and a bitch Brenock's My True Kerry Love. Lines which emanate from Shamrock are Tain, Chermar, Desertsun, Kinsale, Terromari, Sunset Hills, Gilchrist, Riverrun, Glenkerry, Royale, Braemara, Donegal and Erinmore. Lucky Charm gave rise to the Hopping Brook line when he was used on Mocara of Sunset Hills. Harrigan and Hogan of Hopping Brook were critical to Raclee, Glenworth and Shandalee. Kenwood, Briarlyn, Shibui, Rumstick, Spindrift, Kinsale Andover, Butterglow, Clanheath and Waterford all used dogs that go back to Hopping Brook.

Gilchrist is another line that comes down from Lucky Charm

through a breeding to Toby Mug of Sunset Hill. A granddaughter of this breeding, Gilchrist's Dena of Waterford, was basic to the Waterford line which in turn influenced Lontree.

The Amaden line used by a Lucky Charm daughter, Jenny Love of Addison Mews out of Roscommons Uncommon of Sunset Hill, as one of its foundation bitches.

Lucky Charm also appears in the following lines: Slievehoven Elfinstone, Glenkerry, Kuhullen, Erinmore and Brenock.

A full sister to Shamrock and Lucky Charm, Brenock's My True Kerry Love, was the key to the Brenock line. Butterglow, Clanaboy and Cedarcroft go back to Perro through her. Ch. Ar-Mar's Mr. McDuff out of My True Kerry Love was the grandsire of Ch. Bomier's Tammy of County Cork who influenced Westland and Brawic (Wavehill). A daughter of B. My True Kerry Love was bred back to her sire to produce Sweet Molly Malone. Her major contribution was to the Butterglow line through her son, Ch. Duffy Muldoon.

Perro's daughter Muffin's Miss Muffet, out of Katie's Madame Dhu Barry, produced Ch. Lady Colleen of Forest Glen. Crackerjack, Merrimeton, Kenwood, Westland, Hallmark, Harwelden, Lejerdell and Greene Acres go back to Perro through her.

CORNBIN TANJAREEN

Bitch, whelped October 20, 1964, by Kelly of Binheath out of Binheath Pooh-Ella.

Tanjareen was another English import and a half sister to Perro Benito. Her major contribution to American Wheatens was through her son, Tanjybairn. He sired three important bitches: Leprecaun's Golden Heather, Lady Patricia of Windmill and Princess Pegeen of Windmill.

Leprecaun's Golden Heather, bred to Ch. Stephen Dedalus of Andover, CD, ROM, produced by Ch. Raclee's Serendipity. The descendants of Serendipity's son, Ch. Raclee Express West O'Andover, CD, ROM, appear in nearly all of the well-known early lines. They include Briarlyn, Andover, Lontree, Harwelden, Diel-Mar, Crackerjack, Ballynacally, Honeywood, Winterwheat, Merrimeton, Wandersee, Spindrift, Butterglow, Gleanngay and Riverrun.

Lady Patricia's influence on the breed comes down through her son, Ch. Mellickway Crackerjack, ROM. His progeny appear in Crackerjack, Kenwood, Amber, Andelane, Merrimeton, Armada, Bradford, Shibui, Hallmark, Rogue, Domino, Westland, Kuhullen,

Marima and Azlough. His half sister, Ch. Mt. Mellick's Desdemona, started the Royale line.

Lady Patricia's sister, Princess Pegeen of Windmill, was the foundation bitch for Aspen Mill. Her descendants appear in the following lines: Jason, Knocknahilla, Butterglow, Hopping Brook, Spindrift, Clanheath and Glenworth.

BINHEATH CUSHLAMACHREE

Bitch, whelped October 27, 1966, by Binheath Winston of Finchwood out of Kilndown Macushla.

Cushlamachree was the third English import. Her most influential offspring was Lady Gregory of Long Ridge by Grants Hill Yankee Trader. Lady Gregory was the foundation for Butterglow from whom Bundas, Blarneygem, Dandydog, Calebran, Angelica and Holweit arise through Ch. Butterglow's Golden Warlock.

A daughter of Lady Gregory's, Butterglow's Shiela O'Brien, impacted on Claypool, Andelane, Berry Hill, Winterwheat, Diel-Mar, Libra, Glindale, Dandydog, Brearah, Andover, Crackerjack, Kenwood, Domino, Rogue, Kuhullen, Azlough, Bhan-Or, Briarlyn and Westland.

Another daughter of Lady Gregory's, Ch. Butterglow's Dream Weaver, appears in the pedigrees of numerous Andover dogs through her son, Honeywood's Cobby Obby. Ballyhoo, Carlinayer, Brenmoor, Shibui, Doubloon, Shar-D, Hullabaloo and Gingerwood all have Weaver in their pedigrees.

BENNEKERRY BEECHNUT

Dog, whelped December 11, 1966, by Holmenocks Hancock out of Hurley's Lass.

Beechnut produced Berdot's Irish Whiskey, Berdot's Gabriel, Berdot's Goldilocks and a few other Berdot dogs. Irish Whiskey's impact comes down through O'Hagan's Cindy of Ashworth who was the dam of Ch. Koop's Kilkenny of Woodridge, ROM, the sire of Ch. Gleanngay Holliday, ROM. Kilkenny is found in the pedigrees of Gleanngay, Amaden, Waterford, Erinmore, Winterwheat, Harriean, Carrigan and Windcrest. A full brother of Cindy, O'Hagans Shannon of Ashworth was basic to Westland and Marima. Pioneer and Honeywood trace back to Berdot's Goldilocks.

BENKER BELTON

Dog, whelped October 22, 1967, by Holmenocks Hancock out of Hurley's Lass.

A full brother to Bennekerry Beechnut, Belton was bred to Gramachree's Evilin Aruin, and produced two daughters, Ch. Tammara of Balitara, CD, and Brydie of Balitara.

Tammara became the foundation bitch for Legenderry and her progeny are found throughout the breed through her three daughters, Legenderry's Dervorgael and Legenderry's Iollann the Fair by Ch. Stephen Dedalus of Andover, CD, ROM, and Legenderry's Ainlee by Leprecaun's Golden Elf. Dervorgael led to Tain, Chermar, Brearah, Kinsale, Terromari, Jason, Wavehill (formerly Brawic) and Broussepoil. Through Iollann came Shandalee which influenced Chermar, Winterwheat, Diel-Mar, Dawnwind and Candlewood. Ainlee's descendants include Wyndlow, Rumstick, Glenworth, Butterglow, Kenwood, Briarlyn, Whitecrest, Azlough, Westland, Marima, Crackerjack, Harriean, Calebran, Ballyhoo, Merrimeton and Domino.

Bred to Dungarvin of Sunset Hill, Brydie produced Amaden's Katie Love who appears in the Chermar, Kinsale and Desertsun lines.

BLARNEY BLONDIE

Bitch, whelped April 6, 1966, by Holmenocks Hancock out of Honeycub Golden Dawn.

Blondie was the third Hancock offspring to make her mark on American Wheatens. She was the dam of Berdot's Irish Mist, the grandam of O'Hagan's Cindy of Ashworth mentioned previously. Blondie's son Berdot's Bit O'Blarney, was the sire of Lady Tara of Aspen Mill whose grandson, Ch. Butterglow's Orange Herbert influenced Bundas, Blarneygem, Calebran and Legenderry.

Lady Tara produced Ch. Christie of Hopping Brook, a foundation bitch for Spindrift, and Ch. Clancy of Clear Water who began the Clanheath line.

Other Blondie offspring were used by Wandersee, Cedarcroft, Berdot and Riverrun. Riverrun dogs produced the stock for Kenwood and Shibui lines. Gramachree's Cruiskeen Lawn, a Blondie son out of Bourcro Bantry Bay appears in the pedigrees of Stonecroft, Ballynacally, Jamboree, Jalin and Wildflower (Schnabel).

HOLMENOCK'S HELMA

Bitch, whelped January 3, 1970, by Holmenocks Hancock out of Ir. Ch. Holmenocks Hodella.

A fourth Hancock offspring to influence American dogs, Helma's offspring were the Hallmoor dogs. Lejerdell and Windcrest trace back to these lines.

LIMERICK JANE

Bitch, whelped August 10, 1970, by Garryowen Warrior out of Skagh Lass.

A Hancock granddaughter through her dam, Jane was bred to Ch. Shaugnessey of Sunset Hill and produced a bitch, Sunset Hill Krissy O'Berg, a foundation bitch for Tircornel and grandam of Ch. Knocknahilla Pegeen, Knocknahilla Maura and Knocknahilla Nie Noneagh. A litter brother to Krissy, Ch. Sunset Hills Dingle Drummer produced Ch. Glenkerry's Danny Boy, who sired some Kuhullen dogs. The Kuhullen progeny appear in Winterwheat and Elfinstone lines.

HOLMENOCK'S HAPHAZARD

Dog, whelped October 14, 1971, by Holmenocks Horris out of Holmenocks Hamla.

A double Hancock grandson, Haphazard figures in the Knocknahila line of Marie Avallone.

HOLMENOCKS HARFORE

Dog, whelped August 4, 1972, by Freddie Klipper out of Holmenocks Hamla.

Another Hancock grandson, Harfore sired two bitches, Gilchrist's Fiona of Riverrun and Gilchrist's Fineen out of Gilchrist Gal O'Slievehoven. The first, Gilchrist's Fiona of Riverrun produced Ch. Riverrun's Flambe Frost. Her descendants include dogs in the Caleycrest, Windcrest, Rivendell, Merrimeton, and Wandersee lines as well as various Riverrun dogs. Fineen led to Meriwood, Cranbrook and Braemara.

CH. HOLMENOCKS HALPHA

Bitch, whelped May 22, 1972, by Ir. Ch. Eden Prince out of Holmenocks Himca.

The most recent import to have any significant impact on the breed, Halpha arrived in this country in 1972. A Hancock granddaughter, whose sire was a full brother to Faraderry Fairy, CDX, Halpha influenced the Ballynacally line. A daughter, Ch. Ballynacally's Beleek, out of Ch. Abby's Postage Dhu O'Waterford, ROM, produced Ch. Ballynacally's Flamin' Mame out of W.C. of Elfinstone. Mame was Willinbec's foundation bitch. Beleek also appears in Broussepoil, a Canadian line.

Beleek's littermate, Ch. Ballynacally's Brian Boru's descendants include dogs in the Sugar 'N' Spice, Cranagh, Jalin, Tumbleweed and Jamboree lines.

Ch. Ballynacally's Brydie Tyrell, a Halpha/Postage Dhu daughter, appears in Bhan-Or, Grian, Clanheath, Mil-Mear, Briarlyn, Schwind, Mayo, Meirlac and Andelane pedigrees through her daughter Ch. Ballynacally's Eden Princess. Princess was sired by Ch. Gibrien's Merry Gaelic Seamus.

HOLMENOCKS HASCARA

Bitch, whelped January 16, 1973, by Ir. Ch. Eden Prince out of Ir. Ch. Holmenocks Hodella.

A half sister to Halpha, Hascara's offspring come down to present-day lines through some Wandersee dogs. There is little influence on the major lines.

APPENDIX 2

Local Clubs

While the parent club serves the fancy nationwide, other clubs form to serve breed interest on a local level. These groups hold matches and/or shows, offer programs on grooming, training and health and, in general, provide a source for breed information.

The first two local Soft Coated Wheaten Terrier clubs grew out of the trimming controversy in 1971. The non-trimmers formed the Soft Coated Wheaten Terrier Club of Metropolitan New York. The trimmers became the core of the Delaware Valley Soft Coated Wheaten Terrier Club. Once the national club was approved to hold AKC point shows, clubs formed in other parts of the country without a great deal of controversy.

Below is a list of local SCWT clubs with their dates of formation, sanction and/or license. My thanks to Marla Friedes of AKC's Clubs Division for compiling this information.

Connecticut SCWTC	1982
**Delaware Valley SCWTC	1971, 1978, 1982
*Derby City SCWTC	1985, 1990
*Greater Cincinnati SCWTC	1979, 1982
**Greater Denver SCWTC	1975, 1983, 1987
Motor City SCWTC	1984
North Texas SCWTC	1986
**SCWTC of Chicagoland	1975, 1980, 1982
**SCWTC of Greater Milwaukee	1976, 1984, 1989

**SCWTC of Metropolitan NY   1971
*SCWTC of Northern California   1978, 1987
**SCWTC of Southern California 1976, 1979, 1984

*sanctioned   **licensed

Please contact the AKC for secretaries of sanctioned or licensed clubs, the SCWTCA for others.

APPENDIX 3

List of Abbreviations

AKC	American Kennel Club
Am./Ber. Ch.	American and Bermuda Champion
AMCH	American Bench Champion
CD	Companion Dog
CDX	Companion Dog Excellent
CERF	Canine Eye Registry Foundation
Ch.	Champion
FCI	Federation of Cynologique Internationale
INTUCH	International Bench Champion
LP	Swedish obedience title between CD and CDX
NUCH	Norwegian Bench Champion
OFA	Orthopedic Foundation for Animals
SLCH	Swedish Obedience Champion
SUCH	Swedish Bench Champion
TD	Tracking Dog
TDX	Tracking Dog Excellent
UD	Utility Dog

The Wheaten's adaptability to training enabled it to be seen during the breed's Miscellaneous class days by people who otherwise might never have noticed the breed and taken it up. This pioneering pair from that period consists of Gramachree's Minute Man, CDX, shown here working out a broad jump, with Eileen O' Connor Jackson.

The people-pleasing Wheaten makes friends so readily because it fits so well into the lifestyles of dog lovers far and wide. As a companion, as a show dog, as an obedience competitor, the Wheaten has shown itself to be all that could be desired in an all-around fun dog. *Sue Poulin*

APPENDIX 4

Wheaten Owner's Library

All Wheaten owners owe it to themselves and their dogs to read and learn about caring for their Wheatens. Below is a list of books that I have found to be useful. There are some that are out of print, but you may be able to get them from a used-book dealer or at a garage sale. They are worth the effort of a diligent search. While the list is by no means complete, it should serve as a core collection for most Wheaten owners.

HISTORY

Holmes, Maureen. *The Wheaten Years*. Orland Park, Ill.: Alpha Beta Press, 1977.

Horner, Tom. *Terriers of the World*. London: Faber and Faber, 1984.

O'Connor, Margaret A. *Soft Coated Wheaten Terriers*. Neptune City, N.J.: T.F.H. Publications, 1990. (Reissue of her 1974 book, *How to Raise and Train a Soft Coated Wheaten Terrier*.)

Soft Coated Wheaten Terrier Club of America. *Celebrating Ten Years of AKC Registration*. 1986.

Vogels, Cindy, ed. *The Soft Coated Wheaten Terrier Yearbook, 1983–1987*. Boulder, Colo.: Index Publishers, 1988.

———. *The Soft Coated Wheaten Terrier Yearbook, 1988*. Boulder, Colo.: Index Publishers, 1989.

————. *The Soft Coated Wheaten Terrier Yearbook, 1989.* Boulder, Colo.: Index Publishers, 1990.

CARE AND BEHAVIOR

Anderson, Moira K. *Coping With Sorrow on the Loss of Your Pet.* Los Angeles: Peregrine Press, 1987

Animal Medical Center. *The Complete Book of Dog Health.* New York: Macmillan, 1985.

Campbell, William E. *Owner's Guide to Better Behavior in Dogs and Cats.* Goleta, Calif.: American Veterinary Publications, 1986.

Collins, Donald R. *The Collins Guide to Dog Nutrition.* New York: Howell Book House, 1987.

Gerstenfeld, Sheldon L. *The Dog Care Book.* Reading, Mass.: Addison-Wesley, 1989.

Rutherford, Clarice. *How to Raise a Puppy You Can Live With.* Loveland, Colo.: Alpine Publications, 1981.

Soft Coated Wheaten Terrier Club of America. *The Soft Coated Wheaten Terrier Owner's Manual.* 1984.

TRAINING

Benjamin, Carol Lea. *Dog Problems: A Professional Trainer's Guide to Preventing and Correcting Aggression, Destructiveness, Housebreaking Problems . . . and Much, Much More.* New York: Howell Book House, 1989.

Benjamin, Carol Lea. *Mother Knows Best.* New York: Howell Book House, 1985.

Benjamin, Carol Lea. *Second-Hand Dog.* New York: Howell Book House, 1988.

Climer, Jerry. *How To Raise a Dog When Nobody's Home.* Jackson, Mich.: Penny Dreadful Publishers, 1983.

Evans, Job Michael. *The Evans Guide for Civilized City Canines.* New York: Howell Book House, 1988.

Evans, Job Michael. *The Evans Guide for Housetraining Your Dog.* New York: Howell Book House, 1987.

Fox, Michael W. *Superdog: Raising the Perfect Canine Companion.* New York: Howell Book House, 1990.

Wolters, Richard A. *Home Dog.* New York: E. P. Dutton, 1984.

SHOWING

Forsyth, Jane, and Robert Forsyth. *The Forsyth Guide to Successful Dog Showing.* New York: Howell Book House, 1975.

Sabella, Frank T. *The Art of Handling Show Dogs*. Hollywood, Calif.: B&E
Publications, 1980.

BREEDING

Lee, Muriel P. *The Whelping and Rearing of Puppies*. Plantin Press, 1983.
Seranne, Ann. *The Joy of Breeding Your Own Show Dog*. New York: Howell
Book House, 1980.
Walkowicz, Chris, and Bonnie Wilcox. *Successful Dog Breeding*. New York:
Arco, 1985.
Willis, Malcolm B. *Genetics of the Dog*. London: H. F. & G. Witherby, Ltd.:
1989.